THE WORLD OF THE

TOUR DE FRANCE

Stephen Puddicombe

sona BOOKS

sona BOOKS

First published in the UK by Sona Books, an imprint of Danann Media Publishing Limited, 2023
Reprinted with corrections 2025

CAT NO. SON0553

Written by: Stephen Puddicombe
Book design: Darren Grice and Kevin Gardner
Editor: Martin Corteel
Proof reader: Finn O'Neill and Sofia Della Valle
Cover images: Getty Images

Printed in EU

ISBN: 978-1-915343-13-0

PREVIOUS PAGE

Didi Senft, better known as 'Didi the Devil', a German cycling fanatic whose energetic celebrations on the roadside have been a regular sight at the Tour de France since 1993

CONTENTS

INTRODUCTION 8

CHAPTER ONE: THE ESSENTIALS 10

The Basics 12
Races Within Races 14
Riders and Tactics 16
Support Staff and Communications 20
The Bikes 22

CHAPTER TWO: THE CONTENDERS 24

Remco Evenepoel 26
Biniam Girmay 30
Jasper Philipsen 34
Tadej Pogačar 38
Primož Roglič 42
Geraint Thomas 46
Wout van Aert 50
Jonas Vingegaard 54
Adam Yates 58

CHAPTER THREE: THE TEAMS 62

Alpecin-Deceuninck 64
Red Bull-Bora-Hansgrohe 66
EF Education-EasyPost 68
Groupama-FDJ 70
Ineos-Grenadiers 72
Jayco-AlUla 74
Lidl-Trek 76
Movistar Team 78
Soudal-Quick-Step 80
Team Visma-Lease a Bike 82
UAE Team Emirates 84

CHAPTER FOUR: THE TRADITIONS 86

The Yellow Jersey 88
The Green Jersey 90
The King of the Mountains 92
The White Jersey 94
The Grand Départ 96
The Champs-Élysées Finale 98

CHAPTER FIVE: THE MOUNTAINS 100

Alpe d'Huez 102
Col d'Aubisque 104
Col du Galibier 106
Col d'Izoard 108
Col Tourmalet 110
Hautacam 112
Mont Ventoux 114
Puy-de-Dôme 116

CHAPTER SIX: THE HISTORY 118

The Early Years 120
The Post-War Years 122
The Merckx Era 124
The Hinault Era 126
The Induráin Era 128
The Armstrong Era 130
The British Era 132
Mark Cavendish: Record Breaker 134

THE RECORDS 138

Stephen Puddicombe is a freelance cycling writer and has written for various outlets over the last ten years, including *Cycling Weekly, Cyclingnews, Rouleur, Velonews, Cycle Sport* and *Tour* magazine. He specialises in road racing, and remains as passionate as ever about the sport he grew up watching.

Every July, the sporting world turns its attention towards France for an event that has, over the course of its long history, become infamous as a gruelling test of human endeavour, and for its great prestige and esteem – the Tour de France. Since first being held in 1903 as part of a publicity stunt hosted by a newspaper trying to sell more copies, the Tour has grown to become the world's biggest annual sporting event. Now, millions of spectators take to the roadside to watch the race go by, with many more millions watching the event on TVs all around the world. Now over one hundred years old, it has become so much more than just a bike race, but a national institution, with a wealth of history and culture attached to it, and which people know even without an interest in sport.

NTROD

In this guide, we'll dive into the world of the Tour de France and talk about everything that makes it so special. We'll talk about the contemporary stars who undertake the superhuman efforts required to become champions of the Tour, and the teams that they ride for; the many icons and traditions associated with the race, from the yellow jersey to the Champs-Élysées; and the rich history of the sport, from old legends that have been passed on from generation to generation since the race's early days, to the controversies and scandals that have rocked it over the years. And, as it's not the more intuitive sport for a beginner to get to grips with, we'll also explain the basics of how bike racing works and what the tactics are, to help illuminate the many nuances that go alongside the physical undertakings of a sport that's sometimes referred to as 'chess on wheels'.

UCTION

THE ESS

Bike racing has its own codes, customs and tactics, all of which contribute to making it one the most nuanced, interesting sports there is. To understand exactly what's going on at the Tour de France, therefore, it's handy to know some of the basics, and to gain a deeper understanding for the many fascinating complexities. How does the Tour de France work? What's the difference between winning a stage and winning the yellow jersey? Do competitors ride as individuals, or as part of a team? Read on for answers to these and many more questions.

ENTIALS

THE BASICS

The Tour de France may not be the only bike race of the season, but it is without doubt the biggest. Other road races take place throughout the whole year save for a break in the winter, including an elite World Tour schedule of thirty or so of the most illustrious races. But in terms of prestige and world-renowned, the Tour stands alone.

Normally starting during the first week of July, the Tour is one of only three races to last three weeks, along with the Tours of Italy and Spain (or, in their native tongue, the Giro d'Italia and Vuelta a España). Because of their extreme length these races are known as the 'Grand Tours' of cycling, but there are many shorter multi-day 'stage races' as well as single-day 'classics' that take place all around the world, all to varying degrees of importance and notoriety.

Different riders target different races in the season, but the Tour de France attracts most of the world's very best. A total of 176 riders participate, divided into 22 teams of eight, of which 18 gain guaranteed admission for being a part of cycling's elite World Tour level, and another four are given wildcard selections, chosen at the behest of the race organisers ASO (Amaury Sport Organisation).

The route varies each year, but with some constants. There are always a few stages in mountain ranges of the Alps and the Pyrenees, where the most important battles for overall victory take place, and the Tour always finishes in Paris along the Champs-Élysées boulevard. Beyond that, it's up to ASO, and the Tour race director Christian Prudhomme, to decide and work out how to get the race to Paris each year. Three weeks isn't enough to cover every region of the nation, considering how few stages last longer than 200 kilometres in the modern era, and that large transfers in between stages are disliked for logistical reasons. From the blustery conditions of Brittany coastline, to the heat of the French Riviera, to the hills of the Massif Central, each area poses its own unique challenges, and contributes to the variety of landscapes and demands that makes a Tour de France.

2025 TOUR DE FRANCE ROUTE

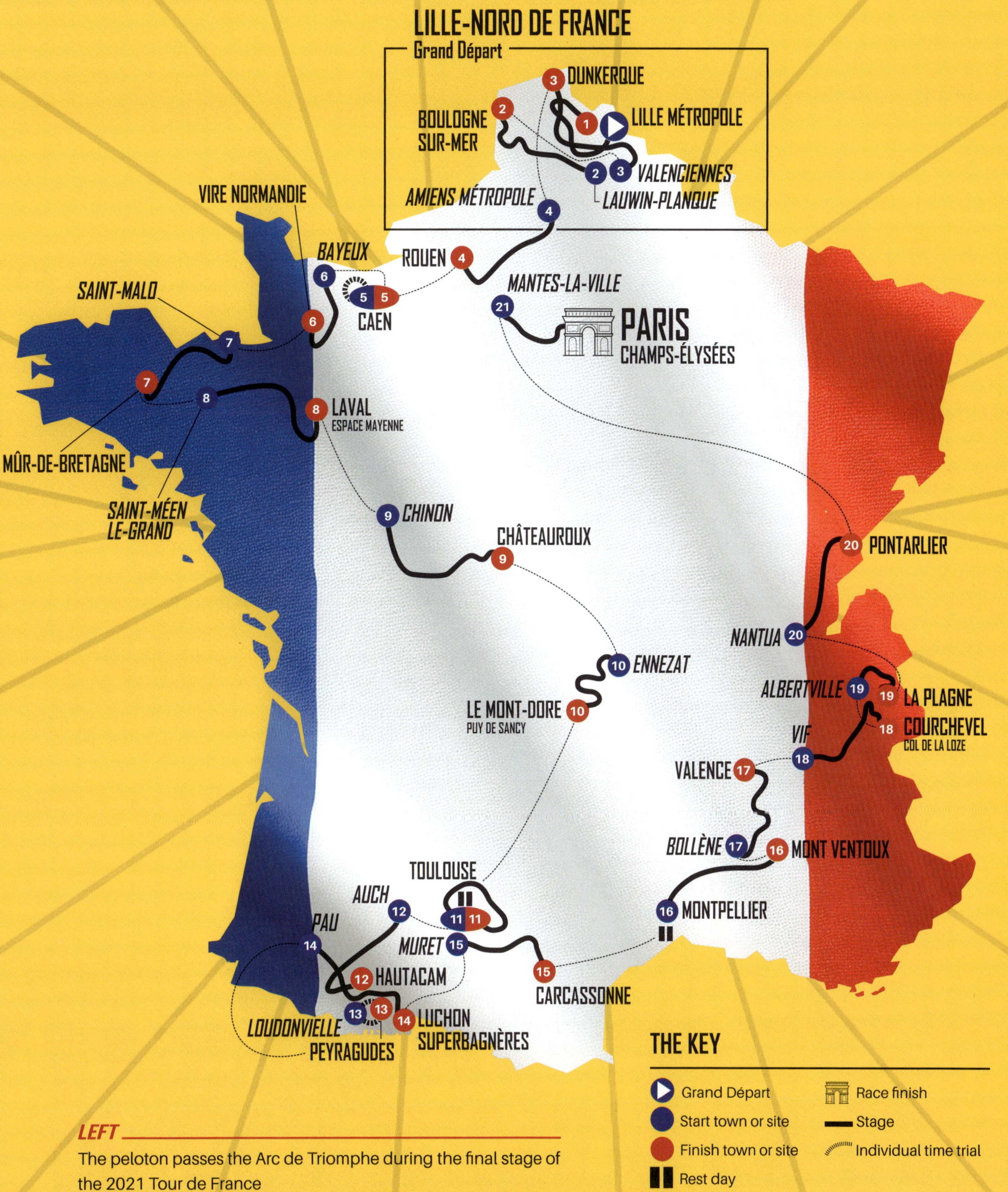

LEFT

The peloton passes the Arc de Triomphe during the final stage of the 2021 Tour de France

RACES WITHIN RACES

The ultimate prize at the Tour de France is the yellow jersey, awarded to the winner of the General Classification (the 'GC'). Cycling is in many ways a complex sport, with many nuances and tactical variations, but the fundamentals of the GC are simple: whichever rider completes the Tour de France in the least amount of time is crowned the winner. Finishing second and third fastest will earn a rider an esteemed place on the podium, while any ranking down to tenth is considered a significant achievement.

Beyond this race for the overall classification are many more races within the race, that ensure the Tour is more than just the contest for the yellow jersey. After all, the Tour de France is a race that lasts three weeks, and is made up of 21 daily individual stages, each one offering plenty of prizes to play for. Above all, being the winner of an individual stage, and getting to cross the line with your arms aloft in celebration, brings with it immediate satisfaction and success. While some riders play the long game and prioritise finishing high on the GC above all else, others spare no thought for their overall time, and focus instead on targeting specific stages to try and win. You can even finish rock bottom of the GC, or not even make it to the finish of the Tour in Paris, and still have a successful race if you can manage to win a stage.

As well as the yellow jersey, there are other classifications that unfold over the course of the race, and are only concluded when the race finishes Paris. The green jersey denotes the leader of the points classification, a competition based on the finishing position of each stage rather than time. As there are more flat stages than mountainous stages in the Tour, this competition is contested by riders who do well in that terrain: sprinters. The polka-dot jersey, meanwhile, is for the King of the Mountains, for which riders acquire points by being among the first to the summit of climbs. These climbs are categorised in terms of difficulty, 4 being the lowest and 1 the highest, with the exception of the even harder 'hors' category, translating as 'beyond classification '; the harder the climb, the more points are awarded. All of these jerseys are highly sought after, and simply leading the classification at any point in the race and therefore getting to wear the jersey is considered a great honour.

ABOVE

A bloodied Christian Vande Velde after a crash during the 2010 Tour de France

LEFT

The polka-dot jersey, yellow jersey, green jersey and white jersey all wait at the start of a stage of the 2020 Tour de France

BELOW
A race radio, the device used for team managers and directeurs sportif to communicate with their team's riders during a race

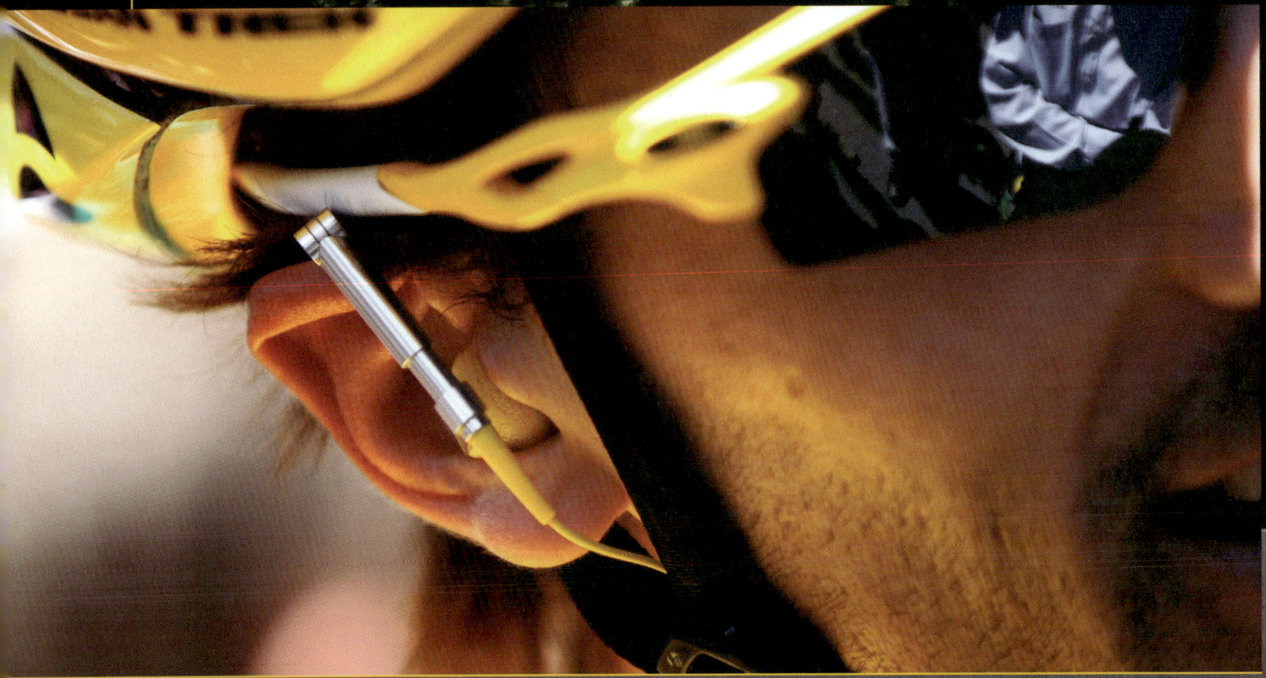

RIDERS AND TACTICS

Within a Tour de France are a variety of different types of stages, each with different kinds of 'parcours' (or terrain) that suit different kinds of riders. Although those competing for the yellow jersey have to be careful to remain alert on each day of the race, there are two types of stages that are especially important, and generally determine the eventual outcome: mountainous stages, and individual time trials. Why? Because these are the stages in which there are the largest time gaps between riders. The harder the climb, the more selective it is, and greater the distances between riders, therefore mountainous terrain is where the top 'climbers' are able to gain significant time in the contest for overall victory. And in time trials, each rider sets off individually to complete a course as quickly as possible. Without being able to ride in groups, as they would for most normal stages, significant differences open up between contenders. To win the yellow jersey, therefore, one has to be an elite climber, but generally not a 'pure' climber who will lose too much ground in the time trials.

Mountainous stages and time trials may be the most important stages in terms of the general classification, but the most common type are flat stages, which are generally won by 'sprinters'. As there is less in the parcours to separate the riders, the riders tend to stay together in one large bunch, known as the 'peloton', for most of the stage, and the winner is decided by a mass sprint between them. Sprinters are usually larger and stockier than the GC contenders, as they specialise in short-term bursts of accelerations rather than steady and long efforts. And they also have to have great bike-handling skills and nerves of steel, as these bunch sprint finishes, and the kilometres that precede them, are chaotic affairs in which there are always risks of

MAIN IMAGE
Team Sky riding in unison at a team time trial stage during the 2018 Tour de France

crashes. GC contenders have to be careful throughout a stage not to crash, and keep out of the way at the finish while the sprinters duke it out for victory so as to minimise the risk.

In between the mountainous stages on one end of the spectrum and flat stages on the other extreme are various 'hilly' or 'intermediate' stages. Sometimes these stages can be just about difficult enough for the GC riders to try to gain time over each other, or easy enough for the sprinters who are decent at climbing to try and stay in contention for a sprint finish contested by a reduced peloton, shorn of the sprinters who are less capable. But often these are won by a mixture of 'puncheurs', who are able to produce powerful accelerations on shorter hills, and 'breakaway specialists', who can pick the right moment to break out of the peloton, and have the power to stay clear and ride to victory. And when hills aren't the decisive factor, sometimes strong winds can wreak havoc on a stage, where heavier, more powerful riders are able to put the lighter ones under pressure. These are rare occurrences, but, when the wind does blow strong enough and in the right direction (usually 'crosswinds' from the side, which forces riders into an 'echelon' formation and makes it very difficult to keep hold of the wheel of the riders ahead), the results are thrilling, in terms of both the battle for the stage win and that for the overall victory.

Most stages of the Tour de France, whatever the terrain, tend to follow the same pattern: several riders 'attack' out of the peloton at the start of the day until a 'breakaway' group is formed, which the peloton at some point later begins to 'chase' by increasing the pace in an attempt to bring them back before the finish. On flat stages the breakaway group has a low chance of succeeding, as it's much easier to ride in a large group in such terrain (due to not being as exposed to the wind), and therefore it tends to be populated by weaker, less heralded riders from smaller teams, aware of how low the odds of them winning are, but taking the opportunity of publicity and get their team kit some valuable television coverage. On hillier and more mountainous stages, however, these breakaways tend to be of higher calibre, as riders sense a greater likelihood of a breakaway making it to the finish without being caught.

An 'attack' is when a rider suddenly accelerates in order to break out of the group they are currently in. Whether made in order to attempt to win a stage, or to gain an advantage in the GC race, there are many tactical considerations to take into account. An attack early in the stage is normally considered risky, as it requires a large, fatiguing effort to sustain that could prove costly later. But leave it too late to attack, and you may either have missed the opportune moment, or, if trying to gain time, have run out of road to gain a significant advantage. The big GC gains are made with these attacks, but one can also sustain significant losses by being 'dropped'. This is when a rider finds the pace of a group too hard to handle, and falls behind.

Another integral element of cycling tactics is the role played by teammates. Although races are won by individuals, they are raced as part of a team, and a harmonious hierarchy in which every rider knows their role within the team is essential. Each team has a 'leader' (sometimes multiple leaders) who is considered the team's best chance of success, and therefore is protected by the other riders in the team, who sacrifice their own personal chances in order to maximise that of their leader. These riders are known as 'domestiques' (which translates as 'servants', and, depending on their skillset, there are many different ways in which they can be of service; be it riding at the front of a group in order to try and chase a breakaway, looking after and 'leading-out' a sprinter in the hectic final few kilometres of a bunch sprint finish, or setting a desired-for pace up a climb with their leader on their wheel.

ABOVE

Mark Cavendish, dressed in the rainbow jersey worn as world champion, celebrates winning the final stage of the 2012 Tour de France

MAIN IMAGE

The peloton climbs the Col du Lautaret during the 2022 Tour de France, one of the huge summits of the Alps

SUPPORT STAFF & COMMUNICATIONS

If you ever watch the Tour de France pass by on the roadside, you'll notice just how much more there is to the race than just the couple of hundred cyclists taking part. So many cars, motorbikes and even helicopters accompany them on the road that the scene resembles something out of a Mad Max film, and all contribute to the crazy travelling circus that is the Tour de France.

Motorbikes weave their way through the convoy, some for policing and security purposes, others carrying media representatives, including camera operators recording live television footage up close. From over their heads the whirl of helicopters can be heard, providing a wider, birds-eye view of the action for TV. And behind the peloton follows a long, noisy convoy of cars, among them medical professionals on hand in case of injury or emergency, and team cars

TOP

Edward Planckaert takes a bidon from his team's soigneur, waiting for him on the road at the 2022 Tour de France

BOTTOM

Team AG2R La Mondiale motorbike riders monitor progress during stage 18 of the 2018 Tour de France

carrying spare bikes and wheels in case a rider needs to ditch theirs, whether due to a puncture or damage from a crash. A mechanic rushing from out of the car to carry out a swap as quickly as possible is a common sight, and is sort of like cycling's equivalent for a pit-stop in F1.

Also present in these team cars are 'directeur sportifs' ('DS's), the brains behind the operation in every team. Observing the race from the convoy, it's up to these DSs to manage a squad's tactics, and they inform and instruct their riders via a race radio system that each member is wired into via earpieces. Not that riders always take on board the instructions – sometimes they can be seen angrily removing the earpiece during a race.

These team cars also provide the essential service of keeping a rider fuelled during a race, by handing out 'bidons' full of water when thirsty riders drop back alongside them. In terms of food, each squad positions 'soigneurs' at designated 'feed zones' to hand out 'musettes', small bags carrying food for the competitors to grab and eat. Riders are also sure to always have a fast-acting energy gel on hand, too, to avoid the dreaded hunger knock, or 'bonk'. They may not taste great, but they do the job. And if they need a comfort break? If the pace is slow enough there's time to stop and find a spot (which the TV cameras will tactfully look away from), but if not, there's the somewhat cruder solution of spraying the roadside while on the move.

MAIN IMAGE

Gino Bartali hands a wrench used to tighten his handlebars back to his coach in his team car during the 1953 Tour de France

THE BIKES

For enthusiastic amateur bike riders, one of the main appeals of tuning in to watch the Tour de France is the vast array of enviably high-quality tech on display. The Tour showcases the crème de la crème of modern, cutting-edge cycling technology, and the pros are equipped with bikes that make the mouth water.

These modern, lightweight, carbon fibre bikes are a far cry from those used in the early years of the Tour, and the race's history has been one of gradual but constant technological development. The very first Tours were won by riders using steel bikes with fixed gears, and though multiple gears quickly followed they required the rider to dismount and manually change them. Only in the years around World War 2 did derailleur gears become the norm. More innovations followed over the subsequent decades, as gearing became more complex, bikes lighter in weight, and toe clips started to be used.

One particular significant change in more recent decades has been the material bikes are made out of. In the 1990s, aluminium superseded steel as the metal of choice due to its lighter weight. Then, in the 2000s, bike racing entered the reign of carbon bikes, that we are still living in today. Nowadays, bikes weigh in at just 6.8kg, the limit set by cycling's governing body, the UCI.

ABOVE

A vintage seventies racing bike with one fixed gear

Although technology is always advancing, other restrictions are placed on bike materials, and even the way riders are allowed to position themselves on the bike. As well as weight, aerodynamics is seen as a key factor in riding efficiently, and ways are always being devised in order to decrease wind resistance. In 1989, Greg LeMond added handlebar extensions for the final stage time trial, which may have proved decisive in earning the unprecedented narrow eight-second winning advantage over Laurent Fignon for the overall victory. This helped spark a craze for aerodynamics, especially in time trialling, with the Brit Chris Boardman being a pioneer, using innovative bikes and aero sitting positions to win three Tour time trials in the 1990s. There are now all manner of rules and restrictions to keep up with the new trends and innovations, but scientists are always thinking up new methods to make bikes quicker. Who knows what they might look like in the future?

ABOVE

A modern aerodynamic carbon-fibre racing bike

Above all, it's the individuals who fight it out on the road that make the Tour de France what it is. These are the heroes who push their bodies to the limit to have a shot at glory, and whom fans flock to the roadside in their millions to cheer on. There are great rivalries, big personalities, and everyone has different favourites. In this chapter, we pick the brightest stars of the contemporary peloton, and explain what makes each so special.

THE CON

ENDERS

Remco Evenepoel

Few Tour de France debuts were anticipated with as much excitement as Remco Evenepoel's last year. Since taking the sport by storm at junior level as a teenager, it was clear the Belgian was destined for greatness, and he spent the following years delivering on his potential, winning some of the sport's biggest races. Expectations were therefore high at the Tour, but Remco lived up to the hype. He managed to win the time trial stage in the first week, then held on to a podium position for the whole race to eventually finish third overall, defying sceptics who thought he had a weakness in the high mountains by producing superb performances in both the Pyrenees and the Alps. And though he finished a long way behind Tadej Pogačar and Jonas Vingegaard in first and second respectively, there was an even bigger gap between himself and the next best rider in fourth overall. It was undeniable: a new Tour de France star had arrived.

The performance was greeted with delight in his native Belgium. Cycling is a big deal in Belgium, second only to football in terms of popularity, and great pride is taken in their history. For good reason — in total Belgian riders have won the Tour de France eighteen times, a record only France betters. But the last of those titles came way back in 1976, and ever since, fans have longed for an heir to their heroes of old like the great Eddy Merckx. Now, Evenepoel has been anointed as the man to bring the yellow jersey back to Belgium.

The hype for Evenepoel began early, sparked by his astonishing record in the junior scene. Yet he didn't actually take to cycling until relatively late. As a boy, football was his first calling, and he progressed through the age groups at Anderlecht before representing the national team at under-16 level. He had some technical skill, but what really impressed was his endurance — one of his coaches tells a story of a 16-year-old Evenepoel overtaking him during a half-marathon, just one day after competing in a match. In 2017, aged 17, he decided to switch from football to cycling, and, despite a shaky start as he learned how to race in a peloton, was quickly vindicated. After winning a couple of races during his debut season, he caught fire in 2018, winning almost every race he competed in, more often than not by huge margins.

These performances were enough to capture the frenzied attention of the Belgian press and fans, who hailed him as 'the next Eddy Merckx'. Even before graduating to professional level, his fame grew rapidly, to the point where soon he was known simply as 'Remco'. By the end of 2018, while still just 18-years-old, he was marketable enough to even launch his own clothing line.

With fame comes scrutiny, and Evenepoel's personality has been obsessively examined by fans intrigued by this new prodigy and a media hungry for controversy. He's been accused of arrogance, often by older pros indignant at the way this upstart talks himself up and predicts achieving big things. But one man's perception of arrogance is another's of supreme self-confidence, and so long as Evenepoel continues to back up his words with results, he can hardly be accused of hubris.

He turned professional in 2019, skipping the under-23 level altogether, and towards the end of the year he was already winning big races, including a European time trial title and a first World Tour victory at the San Sebastián Classic. The wins came yet more rapidly the following year, including a remarkable four successive overall victories at stage races, before a shocking incident at the Il Lombardia classic in August that halted his hitherto unstoppable rise. While descending a technical downhill road, Evenepoel somersaulted into a wall and fell several feet into a ravine, fracturing his pelvis and bruising his lung. These were serious injuries, but given the severity of the fall, could have been so much worse.

crivit PRO
latexco
vermarc
NAPOLEON SPORTS & CASINO
deceuninck
WINDOWS

Rehabilitation was long and slow, and his return to racing at the 2021 Giro d'Italia the following May appeared to be premature, as he failed to compete for overall victory and dropped out a few days before the end. At this point, it was unclear whether he'd ever be able to fulfil the potential he'd shown pre-crash, given the severity of his injuries. Thankfully, he started to look himself again later that year and started winning races regularly again.

Then came 2022, the year Evenepoel made the leap from being a hyped-up young prodigy to a fully-fledged superstar. He won his first ever monument classic in the spring at Liège–Bastogne–Liège, a first ever Grand Tour overall victory in the autumn at the Vuelta a España, and capped it off by becoming World Champion at the end of the season. It was enough to see him awarded the Vélo d'Or as the best rider of the year, and confirmed that Evenepoel really was as good as all the hyperbole had suggested.

The big wins kept coming in 2023, including a defence of his Liège-Bastogne-Liège title as well as multiple stage wins at both the Giro d'Italia and Vuelta a España, and last year he became a double Olympic champion, making history by becoming the first man to win gold in both the road race and the time trial. Now, as he turns 25-years-old, Evenepoel hopes to take yet another great leap forward by closing the gap between himself and Jonas Vingegaard and Tadej Pogačar in the race for the yellow jersey, and fulfil long dormant Belgian dreams.

RACING STYLE

Remco Evenepoel rides like a man who does not enjoy company. When he attacks, he tends to do so alone, preferring to ride at his own tempo rather than have to worry about others around him. That might seem a counter-intuitive approach considering the advantages of riding in groups and sharing the workload, but it works for Evenepoel, who time and time again wins races by holding off groups trying in vain to chase him. He's able to do so partly because of his incredible endurance, but also for his unique ability to adopt an aerodynamic position on the bike to reduce wind resistance while not sacrificing as much power as other riders. This has helped him overcome the disadvantage of his lightweight frame to become one of the very best time trialists in the world (last year he was crowned both World and Olympic champion in the discipline), while also proving to be effective in the mountains, where he likes to ride at a steady tempo in contrast to the fluctuations in pace of purer climbers.

MAIN IMAGE

Remco Evenepoel riding to victory during stage 7 of the time trial, 2024 Tour de France

BELOW LEFT

Remco Evenepoel as World Champion in 2022

Biniam Girmay

Veni, Vidi, Bini! So goes the rallying cry of supporters of Biniam Girmay, cycling's new superstar who came from the distant land of Eritrea, set his sights on the Tour de France, and last year conquered the race. On the streets of Turin, at the climax of the Tour's third and final day across the border in Italy, Girmay adroitly found space in a crowded first bunch finish of the race, then surged to the line to take victory, leaving all of the world's best sprinters in his wake. It was a breakthrough moment not only in the 24-year-old's fledgling career, but in cycling as a whole, as by doing so he became the first Black African in the race's 121-year history to win a stage.

And Girmay wasn't done yet. More high placings saw him move into the lead of the points classification a couple of days later, and on stage eight, adorned in the colours of the green jersey, he flew up a draggy uphill finish in Colombey-les-Deux-Églises to pip Jasper Philipsen to the line by a fraction. Then the following week, in Villeneuve-sur-Lot for stage twelve, he achieved a third and arguably best win yet, coming from far behind and overtaking multiple rival sprinters to reach the line first, in doing so extending his lead in the points classification to over a hundred points. He suffered a scare in the final week when he crashed heavily just five days from the finish, but managed to ride through the pain and just about hold on to green, making yet more history by becoming the first African winner of a Tour de France jersey.

Historically, road cycling has been a sport dominated by Europeans, and overwhelmingly White. The emergence of generations from North America, South America and Australia have made the peloton more international from the 1980s onwards, but there's a notable dearth of riders from Africa, and a lack of racial diversity of any kind. In fact, Girmay was the only Black rider to compete at the Tour last year. That isn't due to a lack of popularity, at least in a nation like Eritrea. As was clear from the jubilant crowds celebrating his Tour wins on the streets of Asmara, the nation's capital and his hometown, as well as the prevalence of fans adorning the green, red and blue colours of the nation's flag that has become a common sight in bike race across the world. Girmay has become a household name there – an emblem of national pride that has put this small nation of just a few million on the sporting map.

Yet even before his stratospheric rise, cycling was already popular in Eritrea, having been introduced by Italian colonialists over a century ago. Girmay's own father was a fan, and introduced his son to the sport by watching it on TV together. Given the make-up of the peloton, the race must have seemed remote – until the 2015 edition, when for the first time in the race's history Black Africans took part in the persons of Eritreans Daniel Teklehaimanot and Merhawi Kudus, with the former even leading the mountains classification for four days. A 15-year-old Girmay took notice. "Everything changed when Teklehaimanot wore the polka dot jersey," he reminisced during the Tour last year. "He showed everything possible that gave me a lot of positives that I could also be part of the Tour and win a stage."

It's one thing for someone from Girmay's background to be inspired to become a professional cyclist, but another thing entirely to overcome the many barriers in place. The talent and enthusiasm he exhibited while riding the junior scene in Eritrea as a teenager helped earn him an invite to the UCI's World Cycling Centre, a Swiss-based team designed to provide a pathway to help develop talent, but committing to it required a great deal of sacrifice from Girmay. Signing up involved quitting school and his life in Eritrea to move to an entirely different continent and culture, all at the tender age of seventeen. Girmay was game, though, and excelled enough there to turn professional in 2020, whereupon his results were impressive enough to attract World Tour outfit Intermarché–Wanty to sign him up the following summer.

Within months of that move he made a name for himself internationally at the World Championships in Leuven, where he sprinted for second-place in the under-23 road race to take the silver medal. Then the following year, in 2022, he made the leap from exciting talent to one of the world's elite riders. First came victory at the Gent-Wevelgem, one of the most important cobbled classics on the spring calendar. A month later he made his Grand Tour debut at the Giro d'Italia, where he went toe-to-toe with superstar Mathieu van der Poel during the first week, eventually beating him in a sprint at the start of the second week to win stage ten, and seal another career landmark.

Girmay was, in a quite literal sense, a victim of his own success – when opening the celebratory bottle of prosecco on the podium that day, the cork flew off and hit him in the eye, hurting him enough to have to leave the race the day after. That freakish incident was the start of a run of bad luck and injuries that affected the rest of his season, and continued into 2023, during which he failed to make much of an impression at his Tour de France debut. 2024 started in a similar fashion, as crashes curtailed his classics campaign and forced him to again abandon the Giro. By the eve of the Tour de France that year, his star had dimmed to the point where he'd been usurped by teammate Gerben Thijssen as Intermarché-Wanty's designated sprinter for the race. But then Thijssen crashed in the finale of the first sprinter stage, Girmay stepped up to deputise, and the rest is history.

Sometimes it can feel as though Girmay is carrying on his shoulders not only the weight of a country, but a whole continent. Yet he remains an easy-going, phlegmatic figure, who never betrays any sign of being under pressure. With a temperament like this, the trappings of fame won't stop him from conquering still more of the sport's frontiers.

RACING STYLE

As quick as he is in the sprints, Girmay's real strengths lie in his versatility and consistency. He's adept at staying calm and surfing wheels in the chaos of a bunch finish, and rarely is caught out in the wrong position. He's also able to be competitive in stages beyond just the flat ones, able to do well in classics-type terrain like cobblestones, as well as hillier days. Above all, it's the slightly uphill finishes, like the one in Colombey-les-Deux-Églises where he claimed his second Tour stage last year, that he really excels at, where his slightly lighter frame gives him an advantage against the purer sprinters.

These attributes make him an ideal competitor for the green jersey, and reminiscent of Peter Sagan, one of the most successful cyclists of the 2010s. "I like Peter Sagan," Girmay has said, "not only for his cycling but also outside of cycling. He's really funny and easy-going." This summer, the Eritrean will strive to become the first man since Sagan six years ago to defend his green jersey title, and underline his credentials as his successor.

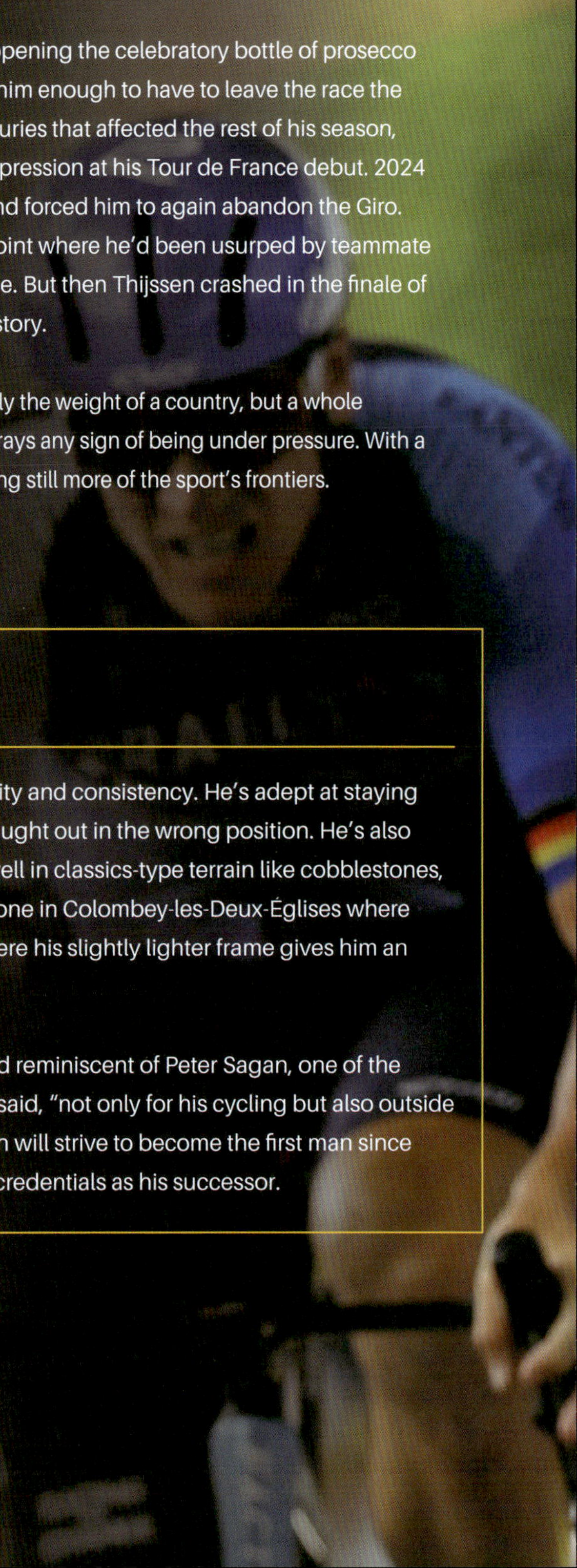

MAIN IMAGE
Wearing the green jersey, a fired-up Biniam Girmay crosses the finish line first on stage 12 of the 2024 Tour de France

Jasper Philipsen

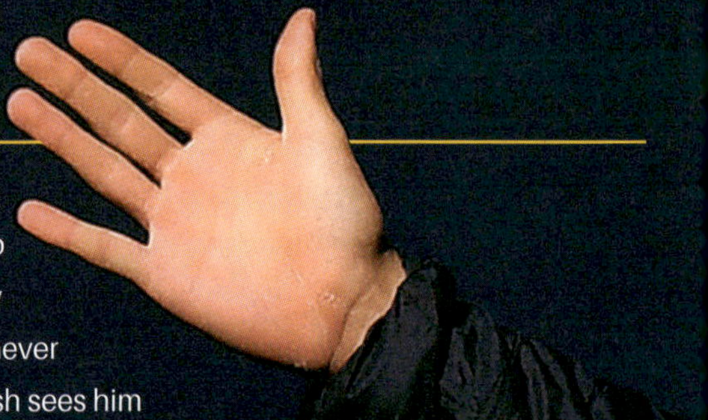

Introducing Jasper Philipsen, the fastest cyclist in the world right now. When it comes to the final few hundred metres of a flat stage, when the sprinters rev up their engines ready to hit top speed for the final dash to the line, there is simply nobody in the peloton who can match the explosive speed of Philipsen. He'll never climb well enough to compete for the yellow jersey, but his peerless sprint finish sees him stage win after stage win. That has been the case in both of the last two Tours de France, in which Philipsen has collected a bounty of seven stage wins. The first half of the 2023 Tour was especially spectacular, as he obliterated the opposition in a sensational run of bunch sprints. He took successive victories in both the first two bunch finishes of the race on stages three and four, deposited at the front each time by lead-out man Mathieu van der Poel and accelerating with enough power that nobody could pass him. The sprint finish three days later wasn't quite so straightforward, as Mark Cavendish nearly caught him out by starting his sprint early, but Philipsen still had the power to come from behind and storm past him for another victory.

These sprints weren't without controversy. Commissaires had to review video replays for a couple of them before clearing Philipsen, following protests from disgruntled opponents that he'd deviated dangerously from his line, and for the other Van der Poel was sanctioned for bumping into a rider during his lead-out. And some questioned whether Philipsen really was the quickest sprinter, or if he was merely piggy-backing off the exceptional work done by Van der Poel. There could be no such doubt after the following sprint in Moulins on stage eleven. On this occasion Philipsen had to do it all himself after an ill Van der Poel was dropped, yet managed to skillfully navigate wheels and come from far behind to once again leave his rivals to the dust. It was his fourth sprint win of the race, a haul only the great Mark Cavendish, Marcel Kittel and André Greipel had achieved in the past two decades. And better yet, despite seeing his unbeaten streak come to an end on the final stage through defeat to Jordi Meeus on the Champs-Élysées, he also managed to pick up enough points in the intermediate stages to win the green jersey.

A difficult start to the 2024 Tour prevented him from defending that green jersey title, as a high-speed crash during the race's first bunch sprint, then a relegation for dangerous sprinting three days later, saw him fall many points adrift of leader Biniam Girmay. It was an exasperating experience for someone who'd enjoyed such uninterrupted success twelve years before, but he showed great resilience by bouncing back in thrilling fashion during the second and third week of the race. First he capitalised on an exemplary lead-out from his team to win stage ten in Saint-Amand-Montrond, then navigated crosswinds and a late crash to take another in Pau, and finally completed a three-stage haul in Nimes with a comprehensive sprint win. Despite the slow start, it ended up being another abundant Tour.

Philipsen had long been tipped to reach such heights. Having stormed through the youth ranks, quitting his physiotherapy studies to commit to cycling full-time, he turned pro in 2018 at the age of just 19. Only a year later he made his Tour de France debut, where, despite being the youngest rider in the race, he still managed multiple top ten finishes in the sprints. Then at his next Grand Tour appearance the following year at the Vuelta a España (now riding for the Alpecin-Deceuninck team), he claimed a breakthrough stage win.

Such a rapid rise was always likely to hit a setback eventually, and the 2021 Tour de France proved to be a frustrating experience for Philipsen. His form earlier in the season suggested he was poised for a career first Tour stage win, but, though he was indeed

UAE
TEAM
Emirates

among the best sprinters in the race, he found himself constantly denied victory by a resurgent Mark Cavendish. Upon ending the race in Paris with yet another runner-up finish (his third of the race, in addition to three third-place finishes) the pent-up exasperation accumulated during three weeks of near misses overwhelmed him — sat on the curbside of the Champs-Élysées, with a celebratory champagne glass in one hand for having completed the Tour, he burst into tears.

In the Netflix documentary series *Tour de France: Unchained*, it was revealed that Philipsen is nicknamed 'Jasper Disaster' in the team for his tendency towards forgetfulness and being a bit of a klutz. He did nothing to dispel that reputation upon his return to the Tour de France in 2022, when he celebrated winning the bunch sprint at the end of stage four, apparently forgetting that he was only sprinting for second-place as Wout van Aert had escaped up the road earlier to take the win. It was an embarrassing moment, and, as yet another runner-up finish, must have left Philipsen wondering whether he would ever win a Tour de France stage. Thankfully, the following week in Carcassonne, he at last took the prize he wanted, edging Van Aert in a bunch sprint to win stage fifteen. Tears were again shed at the finish, but this time of joy.

That victory opened the floodgates for Philipsen, who also won on the Champs-Élysées to add a second stage victory, before adding another seven over the next two Tours to take his career tally to nine. Not content to rest on his laurels, Philipsen wants to keep on winning, and could become not only the best sprinter in the world right now, but the best of this generation.

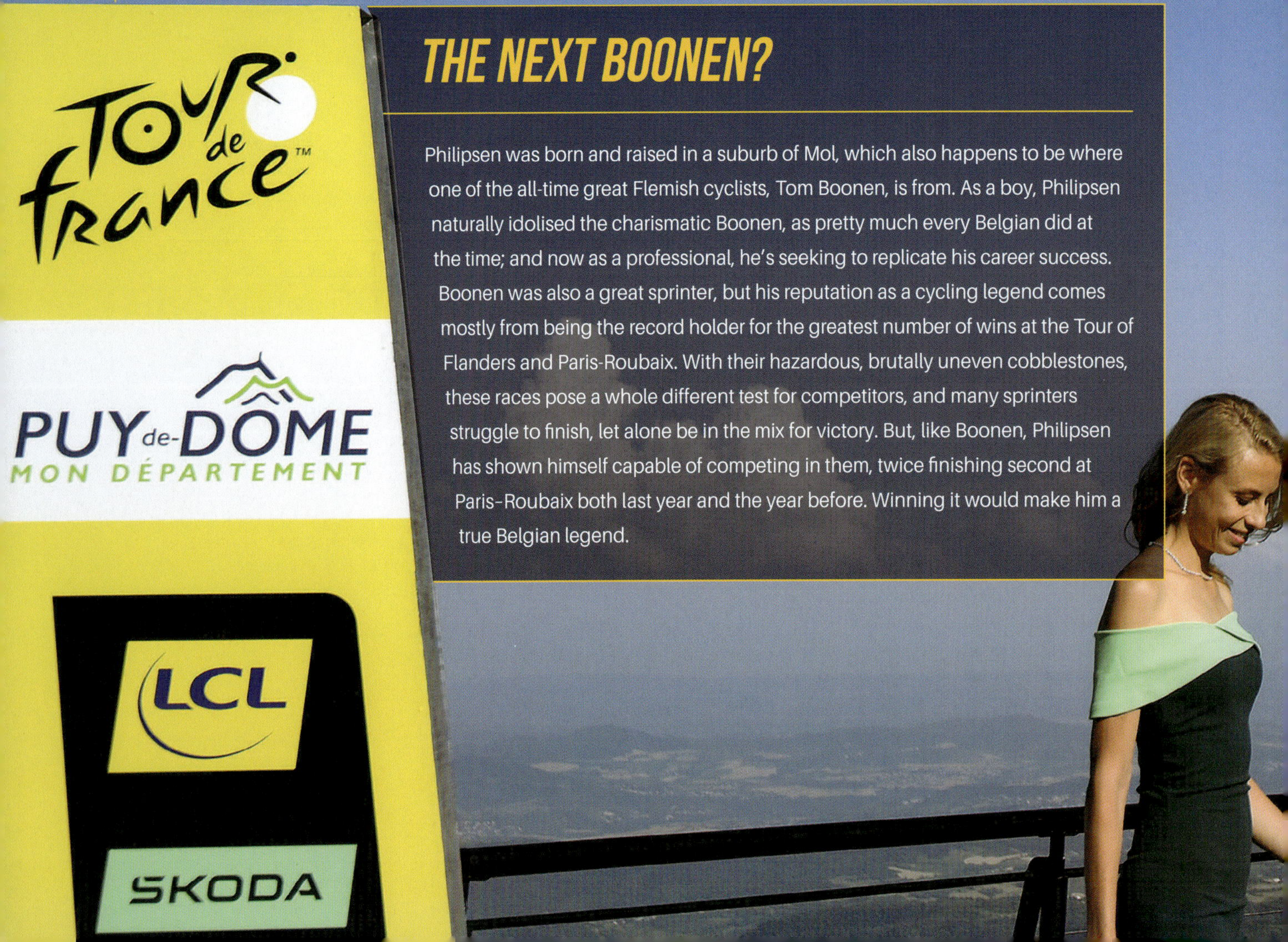

THE NEXT BOONEN?

Philipsen was born and raised in a suburb of Mol, which also happens to be where one of the all-time great Flemish cyclists, Tom Boonen, is from. As a boy, Philipsen naturally idolised the charismatic Boonen, as pretty much every Belgian did at the time; and now as a professional, he's seeking to replicate his career success. Boonen was also a great sprinter, but his reputation as a cycling legend comes mostly from being the record holder for the greatest number of wins at the Tour of Flanders and Paris-Roubaix. With their hazardous, brutally uneven cobblestones, these races pose a whole different test for competitors, and many sprinters struggle to finish, let alone be in the mix for victory. But, like Boonen, Philipsen has shown himself capable of competing in them, twice finishing second at Paris-Roubaix both last year and the year before. Winning it would make him a true Belgian legend.

MAIN IMAGE
Jasper Philipsen on the podium wearing the green jersey at the 2023 Tour de France

LEFT
Jasper Philipsen during the 2023 Tour de France

Tadej Pogačar

There was never meant to be another Eddy Merckx. Cycling's official Greatest of All Time enjoyed such astronomical success during his career in the 1960s and 1970s that every future star that was labelled his heir, however brilliant, could never hope to replicate his achievements. Until now. In 2024, Tadej Pogačar had a prolific, all-conquering, record-making season that would make even Merckx himself blush. As well as winning the Tour de France (the third of his career) he also triumphed at the Giro d'Italia, becoming the first man in 26 years to do a double that had widely been considered impossible in the demands of modern cycling. And, like Merckx, his greatness wasn't limited to the Grand Tours, but extended to one-day races too, with victories at the elite Liège-Bastogne-Liège, Il Lombardia and World Championships among his enormous season haul. Now the question is no longer whether Pogačar is the best cyclist in the world; it's whether he's the best of all time.

Born in Komenda (a suburb of Slovenia's capital, Ljubljana) to Marjeta (a French tutor) and Mirko (an industrial designer), Pogačar developed a passion for cycling when he was nine, and enjoyed success upon entering the junior ranks as a teenager. It was clear as early as his first season as a professional in 2019, when he finished on the podium during his Grand Tour debut at the Vuelta a España, that this easy-going Slovenian was a special talent. But the world still wasn't quite prepared for what he did at the Tour de France the following year. He began the race as an outside favourite, and was given some leeway by the other contenders who allowed him to attack and win two mountain stages, one in the Pyrenees and one in the Alps. By the final week he had moved up to second overall on the general classification, but the 59 second deficit he had to make up to defeat his Slovenian compatriot and mentor Primož Roglič ahead of the final, decisive time trial was deemed by most pundits to be insurmountable. What happened next is history: Roglič floundered, Pogačar stormed to an enormous victory, and wound up winning with a whole minute to spare, becoming, at the age of just 21, the youngest man in over a century to win the yellow jersey.

If this first Tour victory was that of an upstart snatching success at the final hurdle, the defence of his title the following year was one of utter dominance from start to finish. He certainly wasn't underestimated this time around, but there was simply nothing anybody could do to stop him. He launched a devastating long-range attack on the first mountain stage of the race, put several minutes into everyone else, and defended the yellow jersey all the way to Paris without ever looking troubled, winning two more stages along the way.

The following year, he experienced his first ever setback of his career. Jonas Vingegaard and his Jumbo-Visma team set a trap for him on the Col du Galibier in the Alps during what was an epic stage, using both Vingegaard and his teammate Roglič to attack him in tandem, and eventually succeeded in both dropping and prizing the yellow jersey away from him. Pogačar spent the next two weeks trying time and time again to attack and drop Vingegaard, but to no avail, as the Dane proved his equal on all terrain. At long last, the seemingly unbeatable Pogačar had been beaten.

Their rivalry now fully established, Pogačar and Vingegaard spent the first two weeks of the 2023 Tour locked in a thrillingly even-matched two-man contest. However, in the space of just two days Pogačar was subjected to two decisive blows, first being crushed in the race's all-important time trial, then being dramatically dropped on the massive Col de la Loze mountain. "I'm gone, I'm dead", he could be heard confessing dejectedly on race radio while drifting away on that climb, a rare and poignant moment of vulnerability from a man who had once seemed untouchable, as he succumbed to a runner

up finish for a second successive year. Some athletes so used to success would have reacted bitterly to defeats like these, finding it difficult to process and accept no longer having things all go their way. But not Pogačar. He was remarkably stoical in defeat, magnanimous in praising Vingegaard, and barely even showed signs of disappointment at handing over his Tour crown. It's almost unnerving how unnerved was, but this is precisely what makes Pogačar such a formidable opponent – his apparent immunity to pressure. As reflected by his sly, mischievous sense of humour and social media usage, and the way he puts on such a show with his long-range attacks and aggressive racing style, cycling for him is above all about fun, and losing isn't the end of the world.

Magnanimous as he was, Pogačar still badly wanted to win, as demonstrated by the way he returned with a vengeance at the 2024 Tour. First taking the yellow jersey on stage four after an attack on Col du Galibier, he extended his lead to over three minutes over Vingegaard and the rest with back-to-back stage victories in the Pyrenees at the end of the second week. Then, to complete a display of utter dominance, he finished the race with three more consecutive stage victories, on the Alpine summits of Isola 2000 and Col de la Couillole, and the climactic Nice time trial, sealing overall victory by over six minutes. It was a performance the likes of which the Tour has never seen before, worthy of the greatest of all time.

RACING STYLE

One word describes Pogačar's attitude towards racing more than any other: aggressive. With his broad shoulders and explosive accelerations, he cuts an intimidating figure on the bike, and loves to attack at every opportunity. While it had been argued that he was aggressive to a fault, and that his was an overzealous approach that cost him two Tours de France, he was vindicated when he regained his title last year riding with the same daredevil attitude. The quality that makes him really special, though, and that puts him in the conversation regarding the greatest of all time, is his ability to do just about everything. He's a devastating climber on both short hills and long mountains, one of the best time trialists in the world, can handle all manner of road surfaces, and even packs a quick sprint finish. Consequently, he's enjoyed much success beyond the Tour de France – not just in other multi-day stage races, but also conquering specialist one-day classics that virtually no Grand Tour rider in recent generations has managed to crossover into, from the dirt roads of Strade Bianche to the cobblestones of the Tour of Flanders.

ABOVE

Pogačar wearing the white jersey of the best young rider of the Tour de France 2023 as he climbs the Col de Marie-Blanque

MAIN IMAGE

Tadej Pogačar with the yellow jersey on stage 11 of the 2024 Tour de France

Primož Roglič

Away from the Tour de France, Primož Roglič has won just about every race he has set his sights on. He's conquered both of cycling's other Grand Tours, triumphing at the Vuelta a España a record four times and adding the Giro d'Italia to his palmarès in 2023; has multiple other stage race victories to his name; has won one of the most prestigious one-day races, Liège-Bastogne-Liège; and is even an Olympic gold medalist having won the road time trial at Tokyo 2020. But the yellow jersey at the Tour de France is the one prize that continues to elude him. And now, having turned 35 last year, he's running out of time to at last add it to his collection.

Roglič is not the kind of character you can write-off too swiftly, however. He is, after all, notorious for having one of the most unlikely and unorthodox backstories in the cycling world. An only child born and raised in the small mining village of Kisovec, Slovenia, he had childhood dreams of becoming a sports star, but not as a cyclist - rather, it was ski-jumping that first ignited his passions. And he enjoyed significant success in the sport, too, being crowned a junior world champion aged 17 among several other titles. Only after he grew frustrated at the limitations of sport that also required him to do odd-jobs part-time, such as sell goods door-to-door and clean shopping malls, did Roglič turn his attention to cycling instead. At 22 - by which age his compatriot Tadej Pogačar had already won his first Tour de France - Roglič entered the sport as a complete novice, not even knowing the basics about clothing and nutrition, or even what the customs were regarding how to relieve your bladder while racing.

It was a risky career move, especially for someone like him from a working-class background. But he showed real talent, and after three years learning the ropes for small Slovenian team Adria Mobil, signed his first World Tour contract with Jumbo-Visma in 2016. Having reached the elite level, his rise accelerated even more. He proved himself a world class time trialist by winning a stage of the Giro d'Italia in 2016, established himself as a rider capable of challenging for the general classification in 2017, then as a Grand Tour contender in 2018 by finishing fourth at the Tour de France, then a Grand Tour winner in 2019 by landing his first Vuelta a España title. In the space of just four years, he'd gone from being Primož Roglič: former-ski jumper, to Primož Roglič: best rider in the world.

The next thing for him to conquer was the Tour de France, and he went into the 2020 edition as the top favourite. He lived up to that status, too, taking the yellow jersey at the end of the first week and controlling the race with barely a hitch for the next two weeks. But then, when on the brink of sealing victory, everything suddenly unravelled. In the final time trial, a discipline he is usually so strong in, he started haemorrhaging time to Pogačar, and a lead that had seemed insurmountable was evaporating rapidly. By the time he reached the finish, cutting an unfamiliarly dishevelled appearance with his helmet wonky and his elbows jutting out awkwardly, he'd lost the Tour de France.

Even though he has continued to win prolifically in other races, all three of his Tour appearances since that dramatic loss have ended the same way — with him crashing out. He abandoned in the first week of the 2021 race after falling on stage three, was upended by a stray hale bale in 2022, and last year hit the deck while well-placed in fourth overall. Those setbacks revealed a vulnerability to Roglič, and have helped humanise him. Where previously he had been almost robotic in his relentless winning, the way he so graciously accepted his

AGU

defeats has seen fans really warm to him. His personality might initially have seemed aloof and curt, but now, as he has got more used to the spotlight, it turns out he is actually quite shy. These days his dry sense of humour, humility, and his peculiar vocal affection of adding "uh?" at the end of most sentences make him one of the most popular cyclists in the peloton.

"I'm also not the guy who speaks loudly and shows off," he explained in an interview with *Cyclingnews* in 2021. "I think people like it when you don't give up and you keep fighting. I think I'm delivering some kind of message, about not giving up, and I think people appreciate that." And he did just that last year, when he bounced back from his Tour de France crash to win the Vuelta a España, a result that proved he still has what it takes to win a Grand Tour - and that he can still realise his dream of winning yellow this summer.

RACING STYLE

Roglič's trademark is to ride tempo up a climb, then unleash an all-out attack inside the final kilometre. He's capable of accelerating so rapidly that he often wins uphill sprints like this, and can gain significant time over his rivals in a flash. His victories at stage races and Grand Tours have been built on these small but regular gains, as well as the large chunks of time he gains in the time trials thanks to his mastery of that discipline. He's still a very good climber, as you need to be to be a yellow jersey contender, but isn't a purist like some of his rivals, and can show weakness on the longer efforts and those at higher altitude.

He's also historically tended to fatigue more than his rivals the longer a race goes on, and has suffered in the final week of Grand Tours - as at the 2019 Giro d'Italia, when he won two stages in the first week and looked unbeatable, only to eventually fade to third place by the end. Consequently, his approach is generally to seize control of a race early on and build as big a lead as possible, then hang on for dear life in the final stages

MAIN IMAGE

Primož Roglič of the Red Bull-Bora-Hansgrohe team celebrates a stage win at the 2024 Vuelta a España. He went on to win the event for a fourth time

LEFT

Roglič time trialling during stage 13 of the 2020 Vuelta a España

Geraint Thomas

To many, Geraint Thomas is the third British winner of the Tour de France, the man who in 2018 followed in the footsteps of Bradley Wiggins and Chris Froome to continue Britain's golden era at the race. But Thomas himself would put it differently – he's the first ever Welsh rider to claim cycling's biggest prize. A proud Welshman, he was born and raised in Cardiff, attending the same high school as national football icon Gareth Bale. He also met his wife, Sara, in the same town, is a passionate fan of the national rugby team, and, if his reputation is anything to go by, has surely frequented most of the bars there, too.

It was representing Great Britain though that he first made a name for himself as a cyclist, as part of the famously successful British Cycling Academy. Having established himself as one of the top junior talents in track cycling, he was recruited into the program as plans were being formed for the Beijing Olympics, and ultimately won gold there as part of the team pursuit line-up. Four years later, he became a double Olympics champion by defending that title at London 2012. A man with a diverse range of cycling talent, Thomas was concurrently also establishing himself in the world of road cycling, and made his Tour de France debut in 2007, where, at the tender age of just 21, he was the youngest participant in the whole race. In the subsequent years he specialised as a classics specialist and, upon signing for the newly-formed Team Sky in 2010, a formidable domestique.

It was after his second Olympic gold in 2012 that Thomas dedicated himself exclusively to the road, and began the gradual transformation into a rider capable of competing for the yellow jersey. Although already an elite time trialist, as someone whose training had been geared towards the demands of the velodrome, Thomas did not yet have the physique to excel in the mountains of the Tour de France. Only in 2015, when he helped teammate Chris Froome win the yellow jersey as his main helper in the mountains, did Thomas really start to look like the real deal, even more so when he returned the next year to help his leader defend his title.

With such success as a teammate, Thomas was now harbouring more personal ambition, but many doubted he had what it took to achieve the same feats as the leaders he'd previously worked in the service of. He had a reputation for crashing, and struggled to put together a sustained campaign to compete for stage race titles without something going wrong. When his first opportunity to lead Team Sky at a Grand Tour at the 2017 Giro d'Italia ended with him dislocating his shoulder and injuring his knee in a fall, such concerns only intensified.

But Thomas proved all his doubters wrong the following year, when he won the Tour de France. This time Froome rode in his service, after Thomas had proven himself to be the strongest of the two with memorable back-to-back stage wins in the Alps, the latter of which he became the first ever rider to win atop the iconic Alpe d'Huez summit while wearing the yellow jersey. Many feared he'd eventually come unstuck, but each day he survived unscathed, until eventually he was able to celebrate on the top step of the podium in Paris – his yellow jersey inevitably complimented by a Welsh flag.

For some riders, among them Bradley Wiggins, winning the Tour de France is both a blessing and a curse, a life-changing experience that can be difficult to adjust to. But Thomas reports this year as being the happiest of his sporting life, and was able to enjoy the subsequent limelight and relish in his success. He's one of the funniest

and most likeable characters in the peloton, and, by all accounts, the life of the party, and he appears just as down-to-earth now as he was before his historic success.

He'd reached the very pinnacle of the sport at the age of 32, but Thomas wasn't done yet, and returned the year after to prove that victory wasn't a fluke. He finished second-place this time rather than first, but was still part of the winning team as his younger teammate Egan Bernal took yellow instead. Then in 2022, just when it appeared as though his days as a Tour contender were over following a couple of leaner seasons, he returned to his best once more, finishing third-place behind Jonas Vingegaard and Tadej Pogačar. The new generation those riders represent might be taking over the sport, but a 36-year-old Thomas was still able to compete with them. He's focused on the Giro in the years since, where he has continued to defy his age with successive podium finishes, but will return to the Tour de France last year – for what will be his last ever appearance before retirement. Whether he chases stages or rides for GC, we can expect him to go out on a high.

A HISTORY OF CRASHES

Whether down to bad luck, lack of concentration, or poor bike handling technique, one constant throughout Geraint Thomas' career has been a tendency to crash. He ruptured his spleen while out on a training ride in Sydney in 2005, and badly injured his hand in 2009 after overshooting a corner on a descent. He rode virtually the entire 2013 Tour de France with a fractured pelvis, and lost a place in the top five of the 2015 Tour after colliding into a telegraph pole. He's even been blown off his bike before by the wind, at the blustery 2015 edition of Gent-Wevelgem, dislocated his shoulder following a collision with a police motorbike at the 2017 Giro d'Italia, and also pulled out of the 2020 edition when he tumbled over a stay bidon. Yet despite all these knockbacks, he has an amazing ability to pick himself back up again, and has only abandoned one of the thirteen Tours de France he's started in his career.

MAIN IMAGE

Wearing the yellow jersey, Geraint Thomas wins atop Alpe d'Huez during the 2018 Tour de France

ABOVE

Geraint Thomas with the flag of his native Wales, celebrating during the final stage of the 2021 Tour de France having won the yellow jersey

Wout van Aert

There are some sprinters who can go as fast as Wout van Aert in a bunch finish, other classic specialists who can rival him in the one-day races, and a select few capable of competing with him in the time trials. But there is nobody else in the world who can excel in every one of cycling's disciplines the way he can. Simply put, Wout van Aert is uniquely special. Though his climbing falls just short of the level necessary to compete for the yellow jersey, his unparalleled versatility made him the resounding winner of the green jersey in 2022, a classification that rewards the best and most consistent sprinters and all-rounders. And on top of that, he's a great team player, and played a crucial role in helping Jumbo-Visma teammate Jonas Vingegaard win his two yellow jerseys.

Neither are Van Aert's talents on the bike limited to just road cycling. The Belgian first made his name on the Cyclocross circuit, ascending to the very top of the sport before winning the world championships title in 2016 as a 21-year-old, and defending it the following two years. By the third win, it was becoming clear that the world of Cyclocross was too small for a man of his talents, and so Van Aert began to focus more on the road. He made a promising start in 2018, establishing himself as one of the top contenders for the spring classics, and continued to improve the following year, leading to a Tour de France debut. And what an emotional rollercoaster that debut turned out to be. He finished the first week in glory by claiming his first stage win in a sprint in Albi, but ended the race in despair just days later after hurtling into the barriers going around a corner during the time trial when seemingly on the brink of winning a second stage.

Van Aert has since described that crash as career-threatening, and his recovery was long and arduous. It was significantly delayed when a mistake made in the initial operation meant he had to go under the knife a second time, after which Van Aert spent five whole days only able to lie down, and it was weeks before he could so much as fetch a glass of water for himself.

Following such a long time out, which was extended yet further when Covid put a pause to racing just as he made his comeback, would we ever see the best of the then-25-year-old again? You bet we would. In fact, he returned in the summer of 2020 as an even stronger rider, winning classics he'd previously only managed podium finishes at, and returning to the Tour in style with two more sprint wins. In 2021, he was even better, winning yet more top classics during the spring, before pulling-off one of the most jaw-dropping hat-trick of stage wins in the modern era of cycling at the Tour de France. First he won a mountain stage that featured two ascents of the legendary Mont Ventoux, by breaking away from the pure climbers. Then during the final weekend, he defeated all the specialist time trialists to win Saturday's stage, then all the specialist sprinters on Saturday in a bunch sprint on the iconic roads of the Champs-Élysées.

Such all-round brilliance seemingly made him a prime candidate for the green jersey, but he'd never bothered targeting it before, citing his duties as a teammate. For even as he was enjoying this extraordinary personal success, he was performing admirable self-sacrificial work in aid of his Jumbo-Visma's pursuit of the yellow jersey, often single-handedly controlling the race for his GC leader as a super-domestique, whether in the flat roads or in the mountains. And his glum expression as Tadej Pogačar snatched victory from Primož Roglič at the last hurdle in 2020 showed just how much team success meant to him.

Nevertheless, for 2022 it was agreed that he would be given some freedom from his domestique duties to also target the green jersey. No team had won both the yellow and green jersey at the same Tour de France since Team Telekom in 1998, so doing seemed a tall order. But somehow Van Aert chased green jersey points without appearing to ever compromise his teammate

LAZER
Red Bull
ŠKODA
ŠKODA
PARIS NICE
ŠKODA

Jonas Vingegaard's yellow jersey ambitions, spending huge amounts of time out off the front of the race en route to another three-stage haul, while always appearing at Vingegaard's side whenever he needed assistance, sometimes rescuing him when his campaign was plunged into peril. Ultimately, Van Aert won the green jersey at a canter, and Vingegaard won the yellow jersey with all the support he needed, in what was simultaneously one of the great individual and domestique performances in Tour history.

Surprisingly, in the two Tours since he has not managed to win a stage. Though he did again play a key role in Vingegaard's successful yellow jersey defence in 2023, his personal success was limited to a couple of runner-up finishes; and last year, injury meant he arrived at the Tour short of his best, though he did still manage a couple more second-place finishes in the sprints. These results reflect a more general trend that has seen him come close but miss out on his biggest targets, but, if he can stay fit, Van Aert could return to winning ways with a vengeance this year.

RIVALRY WITH VAN DER POEL

Not many sporting rivalries begin quite as early as that between Wout van Aert and Mathieu van der Poel. Born within just a few months of one another, the pair first faced off when they were mere boys at the junior level of Cyclocross, and have continued to compete against each other as they rose to become the two best Cyclocross riders in the world, then on the road as elite one-day classics stars. It's a proper rivalry, too, and the pair have often been on uneasy terms, exchanging the occasional barbed comment when the tension between them has risen to the surface. And they've always been extremely well matched, their inseparability best encapsulated at the finale of the Tour of Flanders monument in 2020, in which they rode the entire finale together ahead of the rest of the field, and had to be separated by the narrowest of photo finishes at the final sprint, won by Van der Poel.

That race marked a turning point in their rivalry, when the pendulum swung firmly towards Van der Poel. Whereas previously Van Aert often came out on top to win major classics, such as Milan-Sanremo and Strade Bianche, but since then his Dutch rival has consistently gotten the better of him whenever the pair have gone head-to-head in Van Aert's most targeted races. Van Aert will need to find another level if he's to keep up in this historic rivalry.

MAIN IMAGE
Dressed in the green jersey, Wout van Aert sprints across the line to win stage eight of the 2022 Tour de France

LEFT
Wout van Aert and Mathieu van der Poel do battle on mud during the 2020-21 Cyclocross World Cup in Namur

talent.

He therefore went into the 2022 Tour de France as one of the top favourites, and with an elevated status within Jumbo-Visma as co-leader along with Roglič. That was upgraded to sole leader when Roglič once again had the misfortune of crashing, and Vingegaard relished the role, taking the yellow jersey from Pogačar after he and his team hatched an ambush on the Col du Galibier. Pogačar spent the rest of the Tour throwing everything he could at retaking the jersey from Vingegaard, but the Dane had an answer for everything, and even won the final mountain top finish in the Pyrenees at Hautacam, to all but wrap up a historical overall victory.

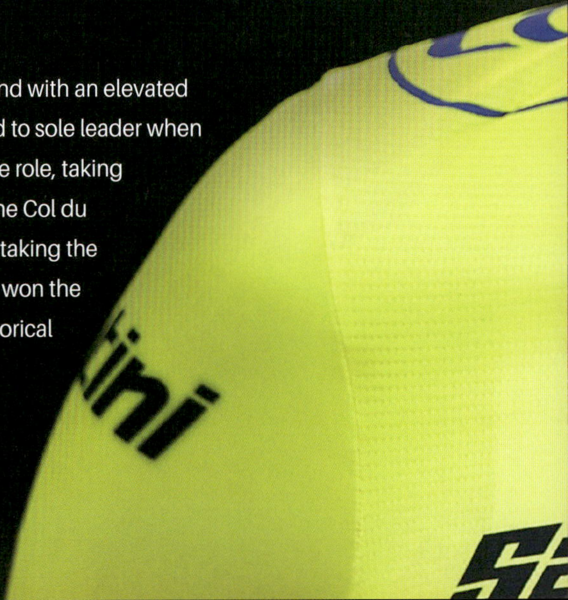

LCL
LCL
LCL
LCL
2022

THAI
Santini
LCL
LCL
LCL

After defeating Pogačar again in 2023 to win yellow a second successive year, his preparations for the 2024 race suffered a severe blow in April when he crashed so severely that he not only feared for his career, but for his life. "I had some internal bleeding that means I'd either drown in my own blood or die from bleeding to death," he admitted in an interview with Danish broadcaster *DR*. "So, yeah... I thought that was the end of it." He survived, but with seven broken ribs, two punctured lungs and a broken collarbone, so it was borderline miraculous that he managed to make the Tour de France at all, let alone be competitive there. Somehow, he recovered enough to once again do battle with Pogačar for yellow, and though his rival ultimately pulled clear in the Pyrenees and Alps, it was apparent from his tears at the finish upon winning a second week stage in the Massif Central just how moved and grateful he was to be back competing at the highest level.

Vingegaard's pale complexion and skinny frame can ostensibly cut a vulnerable figure, but he's made of tough stuff, both psychologically and physically. "I think when I will have some time to reflect on it in a few weeks," he said at the end of the Tour. "Maybe I will be even more proud of second place than the two victories I've had." Rest assured he'll be back fighting to reclaim his title this year.

RIVALRY WITH POGAČAR

Having placed first and second in each of the last four Tours de France, the only time in the race's history that has happened, Jonas Vingegaard and Tadej Pogačar have already established one of the great rivalries in the race's history. And like any good rivalry, they are chalk and cheese in terms of personality and racing style: whereas Pogačar is a fun-loving extravert who loves to put on a show, Vingegaard prefers to keep himself to himself and races much more cautiously and conservatively.

It's a contrast that has made for many a fascinating duel over the years, and that has swung alternatively in favour of one to the other. First Pogačar was the man to beat by winning in 2021, then Vingegaard overtook him by inflicting defeats in both 2022 and 2023, and now Pogačar again has reclaimed supremacy. Despite such high stakes and tension, theirs is a friendly rivalry, epitomised by an incident at the 2022 Tour, when Vingegaard sportingly waited for Pogačar following the latter's crash on a descent during the final mountain stage. But in a strictly sporting sense it's a fierce one, that is already unique in Tour history in terms of how long two riders have had a stranglehold at the top of the general classification for, and looks set to continue to define the race for the yellow jersey for the foreseeable future.

MAIN IMAGE
Jonas Vingegaard is welcomed by his Danish fans in City Hall Square, Copenhagen, having returned from the 2022 Tour de France as champion

ABOVE
Jonas Vingegaard and Tadej Pogačar share a sporting gesture during their battle at the 2022 Tour de France

Adam Yates

Presenting Adam Yates, the best British rider in the peloton right now. While he might not have won the Tour as his predecessors Bradley Wiggins, Chris Froome and Geraint Thomas did, Yates is the only British rider since Thomas in 2019 to be part of a Tour-winning team, when he played a key role last year in securing overall victory for his UAE Team Emirates teammate Tadej Pogačar. One of the very best climbers in the world, Yates was Pogačar's trusty right-hand man in the mountains, who time and time again set such a blistering pace that only two or three of their yellow jersey rivals would remain, teeing up Pogačar to launch his attacks. And, despite riding selflessly as a support rider, Yates still performed well enough individually to seal sixth overall for himself.

Though Pogačar and UAE Team Emirates did not win the yellow jersey the year before, having to settle instead for second place behind Jonas Vingegaard, Yates enjoyed an even better Tour for himself — the best, in fact, of his eight career appearances. Things got off to a spectacular start on the very first day, when Yates attacked in the closing stages of the race, and was accompanied by none other than his twin brother, Simon Yates. It was a touching moment of brotherly synchronicity as the two rode away to the finish together, but, riding for rival teams, they were still obliged to sprint against each other. Adam came out on top, sealing not only the first Tour de France stage win of his career, but also the first yellow jersey of the race, which he went on to defend for four days. After handing it over, he wasn't done yet. He excelled in the high mountains, to the extent that he was riding with, rather than for, Pogačar, as they tried (in vain) to prise the yellow jersey away from Vingegaard. Yates eventually finished third-place overall (just behind his teammate in second), sealing the highest Tour finish of his career, and becoming only the fourth Brit in history to make it onto the podium.

Unlike the three compatriots who came before, Yates was not a product of the British Cycling system, instead forging a path for himself. Though it wasn't for want of trying. Born and raised near Bury, a tram trip away from British Cycling HQ in Manchester, Adam and his brother first got into cycling when their father took them to the velodrome for track sessions with the local Bury Clarion club as boys. At the age of 18, in 2011, both brothers applied for the Olympic Academy programme run by British Cycling; Simon was accepted, but Adam was rejected. The decision could have stung, were Yates not such a level-headed character who has always been unflappable and able to take things in his stride. "I wasn't devastated," he reflected while looking back to that time in a 2016 interview with *Pro Cycling* Magazine. "I knew I could do something but I wasn't keen on staying in England. Racing in Britain didn't suit my characteristics at all. I was still pretty good on a track, and pretty quick for a small guy, but I'm best going uphill. There aren't any races here that finish on climbs."

With help from the cycling scholarship Dave Rayner Fund, he moved to France, where he shone on the junior road circuit. Upon finishing second overall at the prestigious under-23 stage race the Tour de l'Avenir in 2013, he was snapped up by a World Tour team – not, as most young British talent was at the time, to Team Sky. Instead he signed for Australian outfit Orica-GreenEDGE, where he was also reunited with his brother Simon, and remained there for seven years.

He was an instant success, claiming his first elite stage race title in 2014 at the Tour of Turkey aged 23 and first elite classic in 2015 at San Sebastián. Then in 2016, he announced himself at the Tour de France, finishing fourth overall

UAE
TEAM
Emirates

and winning the white jersey as the best young rider in what was only his second appearance. However, he struggled to deliver on that promise the following years, as inconsistency became a problem. He'd look brilliant sporadically, but suffered too many bad days to string together a GC challenge, with 9th place in 2020 being his best subsequent return at the Tour since. In 2021 he decided a change of team was necessary, and ended up at Team Sky (now known as Ineos) after all, finishing the season by finishing fourth overall at the Vuelta a España - his highest finish at a Grand Tour since that Tour de France breakthrough five years earlier.

Still looking to improve, Yates moved to UAE Team Emirates the following year, where he has enjoyed the prime years of his career. He's set to play a crucial role at the Tour this year, as Tadej Pogačar sets out to defend his title against what is likely to be a resurgent Jonas Vingegaard. And, in the event that any misfortune or lack of form falls upon the Slovenian, it'll be up to Yates to lead the team instead. Who knows, maybe Yates could yet become the fourth British Tour de France champion?

CYCLING'S GREATEST TWINS

On the streets of Bilbao, at the end of the opening day of the 2023 Tour de France, Adam and Simon Yates made history by becoming the first pair of twins to place first and second on a stage of the Tour de France. It might sound like a cliché but they appeared almost telepathic in their understanding of one another, both recognising the moment to attack, and riding together to the finish without having to exchange a word.

Though technically fraternal rather than identical twins, the Yates are still uncannily similar. Visually they're hard to tell apart on the bike aside from their differing team colours, and they've very similar personalities, sharing the same mannerisms, laid-back demeanour and matter-of-fact attitude. They've matching riding styles, too, both punchy lightweight climbers, though they've not always been on an equal footing. Earlier in their careers Simon was the more successful one, especially in 2018 when he won the Vuelta a España Grand Tour, but more recently Adam has taken over since moving to UAE Team Emirates.

Perhaps taking note of this, Simon has followed in his brother's footsteps and switched teams this year, to Visma-Lease a Bike. There he will compete at the Tour de France as a support rider, hoping to fulfill the same role as climbing super-domestique for Jonas Vingegaard as Adam does for Pogačar.

MAIN IMAGE
Adam Yates in sprint action for UAE Team Emirates at the Giro d'Italia in 2025

LEFT
Simon Yates just ahead of his brother Adam in a breakaway, during the 2023 Tour de France

As good as an individual star rider might be, they need a strong team to back them up if they're to fulfil their ambitions at the Tour de France. Based around sponsors rather than nations, the situations at these teams can fluctuate from year-to-year, from differing names to a changing roster of riders, but mostly the biggest and best have long been established as the top heavyweights, with their own distinct brand and way of approaching the Tour.

JUMBO
VISMA
JUMBO
VISMA
EAMS

ALPECIN-DECEUNINCK

In their short time on the professional road scene, Alpecin-Deceuninck have taken the sport by storm. Formerly the team had specialised in cyclocross, where they were the home of multi-world championships winners Niels Albert and Mathieu van der Poel. Then, when the latter started steering himself more towards road cycling, so did the team, and by 2019 they had attained second-tier status and were winning multiple classics.

Their Tour de France debut came in 2021, and what a debut it was. The aim was to hit the ground running, and that's precisely what they did, Van der Poel wearing the yellow jersey for six days after triumphing on stage two, and Tim Merlier victorious on the first bunch sprint of the race.

In the three years since announcing themselves in such style, Alpecin-Deceuninck have gone on to establish themselves as kings of Tour de France sprints, with Jasper Philipsen their talisman. Lots of work has gone into perfecting their lead-out train, with even Van der Poel sacrificing his personal ambition to help support him, and they reaped their rewards during the final two weeks of the 2022 Tour as Philipsen was steered to victories at Carcassonne and the Champs-Élysées. The 2023 edition was even more successful. This was the race that Philipsen proved himself as the undisputed best sprinter in the world, enjoying utter dominance by winning four of six sprint finishes as well as the green jersey, invariably being set up perfectly by Van der Poel's lead-outs. The combination didn't quite click as serenely last year, and they missed out on the green jersey to Biniam Girmay, but Philipsen still managed another haul of three stage wins. Once again this year, they will be the team to control the bunch sprints.

Mathieu van der Poel

The son of classics star Adri van der Poel and grandson of multiple Tour runner-up finisher Raymond Poulidor, Mathieu van der Poel comes from cycling royalty, and has lived up to his lineage since moving full-time to the road from cyclocross. He takes after his father more than his grandfather in the sense that his specialities are the classics and cyclocross rather than climbing, but really comparing Van der Poel to anybody else is to do him a disservice – he's a totally unique rider, with a barnstorming way of racing that defies all reason and convention. Put simply, he attacks at moments that for anyone else would be tactically inept, yet somehow has the deep reserves of energy to make them work.

In recent years, he has been utterly untouchable in the classics. A historic treble of the road race World Championships plus the Milan-Sanremo and Paris-Roubaix monuments in 2023 was followed by two more huge victories at the cobbled Tour of Flanders and Paris-Roubaix classics last year, results that put him in the conversation as one of the greatest of all time. We're unlikely to see such performances at the Tour de France, where he generally rides in more of a support role (and hasn't won a stage for himself since 2021), but make no mistake: Van der Poel is among the most powerful cyclists in the sport's history.

RIGHT
Mathieu van der Poel celebrates winning stage two of the 2021 Tour de France, gesturing to the heavens in honour of his grandfather Raymond Poulidor

Alpecin
FENIX
Alpecin
CANYON
LUXAUTO
Alpecin
FENIX
SHAMPOO
MATERIALS
Alpecin
CAFFEINE

RED BULL-BORA-HANSGROHE

For several years, Red Bull-Bora-Hansgrohe was known primarily for being the home of Peter Sagan. The team signed the Slovak superstar ahead of their first season competing at the elite World Tour level in 2017, and as their talisman achieved some of the biggest results of his career here, including his third World Championships title in 2017 and the Paris-Roubaix classic in 2018. Their Tour de France line-ups were built around him, and he delivered to great success, winning a total of five stages and two green jersey titles between 2017-2019.

Yet throughout this time the team was also careful not to become overly-reliant on Sagan, a wise approach that they are now reaping the rewards from since his departure at the end of the 2021 season. At the Tour, they've won multiple stages via breakaways in recent editions, and young sprinter Jordi Meeus was a surprise victor on the Champs-Élysées in 2023. In particular, Emanuel Buchmann's fourth-place finish at the 2019 Tour de France was a breakthrough moment, as it marked the first time the team had really challenged for a podium finish at a Grand Tour. Since then they've continued to register high overall finishes at the Tour, with Wilco Kelderman and Aleksandr Vlasov both placing fifth in 2020 and 2021 respectively, and Jai Hindley seventh in 2023. Now, their focus is set to narrow following another marquee signing on a similarly elite level to that of Sagan: Primož Roglič. Red Bull-Bora Hansgrohe won the hotly contested race to secure his signature ahead of the 2024 season, attracting him with the promise of prioritising his goal to go all-out to win the yellow jersey.

Hopes were therefore high going into last year's Tour, but ended in bitter disappointment as Roglič, having started well to put himself firmly in overall contention, dramatically crashed out of the race during the second week. Thankfully, the team received a significant return on their investment a few months later when he bounced back to win the Vuelta a España, only the second Grand Tour overall title in the team's history (in addition to Hindley's Giro d'Italia win in 2022). Roglič's imperious performance there, as well as the way the team's illustrious squad of quality domestiques controlled the race for him, suggests that they can potentially challenge for the yellow jersey this summer.

Jai Hindley

In 2022, two years after heartbreakingly losing the overall lead at cycling's second biggest race, the Giro d'Italia, on the very last day, Jai Hindley returned with a vengeance to take overall victory there. With that title in the bag, the next step was to take on the Tour de France, and the Australian made his long-awaited debut at the age of 27 in 2023 - to mixed success. Things started great when he found himself in the yellow jersey after winning a stage in the Pyrenees, but a combination of illness, injuries and poor form saw him slowly slip down the general classification, eventually finishing seventh. He returned last year in a support role for Roglič, but was well short of his best form, and would not have been able to compete for a high GC finish even if he had licence to ride for himself. Still, his results in Italy prove that, at his best, he has the credentials to push for the podium.

RIGHT

Australian Jai Hindley of Red Bull Bora-Hansgrohe sprints during stage 7 of the 2024 Tour de France

SPECIALIZED
Red Bull
hansgrohe
BORA
S-WORKS

EF EDUCATION-EASYPOST

When EF Education-EasyPost (then known as Team Garmin) first entered the World Tour in 2008, cycling was in crisis, with a series of doping scandals harming trust in the sport. Led by manager Jonathan Vaughters, the team made it their priority to implement several anti-doping measures, many of which have since become widely used, and are credited with having helped the sport clean up its act. The team also enjoyed plenty of success from the outset, helping to dispel the idea that you needed to dope to succeed. In each of their first three Tours de France they placed an unfancied rider in the top five overall, most notably Bradley Wiggins in 2009. Prior to that performance, Wiggins was still known as a track rider who'd enjoyed great success at the Olympics, but who'd never excelled in road cycling. His fourth-place finish (later upgraded to 3rd after Lance Armstrong was demoted for doping) was the precursor to his overall victory three years later for Team Sky.

It took eight years for the team to better Wiggins' result at a Tour de France, when Rigoberto Urán battled hard to place second behind Chris Froome in 2017. They haven't quite reached those heights at the Tour since, and have recently enjoyed more success chasing stage wins than placing high on GC. But over the years they've won most of the other biggest prizes in the sport, from the Giro d'Italia in 2012 with Canadian Ryder Hesjedal, to four of the five one-day monuments.

Richard Carapaz

Coming from humble origins, Carapaz first started cycling after his father found a bike on a scrapheap one day, in a country with no cycling heritage. Yet the Ecuadorian nevertheless overcame the odds to make it to the very elite echelons of the sport. His big breakthrough came in 2019, when he caught some of the biggest names in the world by surprise to win the Giro d'Italia. Since then he has turned his attention to the Tour de France, winning two stages on debut in 2020 before finishing a fine third-place overall the following year, beaten only by Tadej Pogačar and Jonas Vingegaard. If Carapaz wasn't already a national icon by now, there was no doubting his status after the Tokyo Olympics the following month, where he became only the second Ecuadorian to ever win an Olympic gold medal.

As someone born and raised high in the Andes, Carapaz benefits from a natural aptitude for breathing at high altitude that most of his rivals lack, and as such excels riding in the mountains. Yet just as important as his natural ability is his crafty race tactics, which can sometimes be underestimated thanks to his affable personality.

EF Education-EasyPost signed Carapaz in 2023, and although an opening day crash brought an early end to his first Tour de France for the team, last year he played a starring role, winning the King of the Mountains classification and a stage in the Alps.

RIGHT

Richard Carapaz of Team EF Education-EasyPost injured after falling during stage one of the 110th Tour de France 2023

GROUPAMA-FDJ

The manager of Groupama-FDJ, Marc Madiot, is one of the biggest personalities in the sport. With his impassioned motivational speeches, proud patriotism and eccentric traditionalist values, he's a throwback to cycling's past, someone determined not to lose sight of the sport's origins as a romantic sport of extreme emotions and heroic hardman feats that can sometimes get lost in the modern fixation on cold hard numbers.

He formed the team in 1997 as a group of plucky Gallic underdogs very much in his image. Despite a modest budget, they achieved some success in their early years, the high point coming in 2003 when Baden Cooke won the green jersey at the Tour de France while fellow Australian Bradley McGee wore the yellow jersey for three days after winning the prologue. But it was in the next decade that the man who would go on to define and become synonymous with the team emerged: Thibaut Pinot. His stage win on his Tour de France debut in 2012 produced what remains arguably the most memorable image in the team's history, of a hysterical Madiot bellowing encouragement behind him in the team car, barely restraining himself from falling out of the window.

That moment marked the beginning of a long, ambivalent relationship of Pinot and the Tour. He enjoyed huge success two years later when he finished third overall and won the white jersey for being the best young rider, giving the team its first ever Grand Tour podium finish. But the following years were marked by bad luck, crashes and disillusionment, as the pressure of being his nation's great hope began to take its toll, and he ceded the limelight to sprinter Arnaud Démare, who won stages at the 2017 and 2018 editions. Then, in 2019, Pinot came roaring back to the Tour in the form of his life, and, after winning a stage atop the Col du Tourmalet, even looked as though he could win the whole race – until a freak injury in the final week forced him into a tearful early exit.

After four more inconsistent years in which he couldn't quite fulfil the hopes of his adoring fans, Pinot decided to retire at the end of the 2023 season and settle into a quieter life at the hobby farm where he lives. Without him, the team lacks anyone capable of delivering a longed-for first French winner of the yellow jersey since 1985, but Madiot is a dreamer and will hope that one of his youthful contingent will one day step up to fill the void.

RIGHT
Thibaut Pinot celebrates winning stage eight of the 2012 Tour de France, with team manager Marc Madiot cheering him on in the car behind

FAR RIGHT
David Gaudu at the end of stage 18 of the 2022 Tour de France

David Gaudu

First making a name for himself as an invaluable domestique during Thibaut Pinot's 2019 yellow jersey bid, David Gaudu gradually improved over the years to emerge from Pinot's shadow and eventually become the team's outright leader, peaking in 2022 when he finished fourth overall. Though he has failed to scale such heights since, and the lingering effects of a Covid infection saw him well off the pace last year, his form took a turn for the better last autumn when he placed sixth at the Vuelta a España. His time trialling is a serious Achilles heel, but he still harbours hope of making the podium one day.

INEOS GRENADIERS

Launched in 2010 with a huge budget and even bigger ambitions, Team Sky (as they were then known) began with the specific aim of winning the Tour de France with a British rider within five years. It sounded almost laughably unrealistic at the time considering the developing state of British road cycling, but somehow they achieved it in even less time, as Bradley Wiggins' annus mirabilis in 2012 peaked with him taking the yellow jersey.

That victory got the ball rolling for what would become a decade of dominance for the team, as Chris Froome took over the mantle to ensure they kept on winning the Tour time and time again. He claimed four more yellow jerseys between 2013-2017, putting him fifth on the all-time list of most ever Tour victories. And what was most impressive about this run was just how comfortable these victories were - he and the team were virtually untouchable, and never looked in serious danger of losing out to someone else.

The team's tactics during this time were not for the romantics and didn't win them a lot of fans outside of Britain, but were brutally effective. Their approach was a science-led one, and using numbers and power outputs they could calculate the exact speed to ride to nullify attacks from their rivals, and mechanically deliver Froome to victory. It might not have been fun to watch, but it was rewarding to be a part of, and much of the team's success was based on internal harmony. The team had a big budget, but not big egos, and riders who would have been leaders in other teams were happy to sacrifice their own personal glory in order to aid the collective.

The decline of Froome did not immediately spell the end of Ineos' supremacy. In 2018 he and loyal domestique Geraint Thomas swapped roles with the Welshman taking overall victory, while the following year saw a 22-year-old Egan Bernal emerge to win the team their seventh Tour title in eight years. Against expectations, however, the team has not won the Tour since. Bernal's youth led many to believe that he would dominate the Tour for years to come, but lingering injury problems and a serious crash in 2022 has since seen his star fade, and he has failed to be in GC contention since. Instead, Visma-Lease a Bike and UAE Team Emirates have usurped Ineos as patrons of the peloton, sharing the last five overall Tour victories between them, while Ineos have fallen behind. It's now been three years since they last made the podium, and last year was their most difficult Tour yet with apparent internal tensions and little success on the road. It's up to the next generation of young talent to bring them back to the top.

Carlos Rodríguez

The man tasked with making Ineos Grenadiers yellow jersey contenders once more is Carlos Rodríguez. It was clear the Spaniard was destined for great things when, at the age of just 21, he finished seventh place overall at the Vuelta a España on Grand Tour debut, and he backed that up with an even more impressive fifth place overall at his first Tour de France the following year. He had looked poised for a similar finish last year, only to fall away to seventh, a pattern that has recurred through his career so far - in fact, in all of the four Grand Tours he has competed in to date, he has fallen at least two places on GC in the final third of the race. At the youthful age of just 24, he still has plenty of scope to improve, and become a fully-fledged yellow jersey candidate.

BELOW
Ineos Grenadiers cross the finish line of the Champs-Élysées at the end of the 2015 Tour de France, having sealed the yellow jersey for Chris Froome

JAYCO-ALULA

In 2012 Team Jayco-AlUla were inaugurated into the World Tour to become the sole Australian representatives at cycling's highest level, and in true Aussie fashion they announced themselves in brash, fun-loving style. Off the bike they drew attention for their lip-synching viral videos, covering everyone from Carly Rae Jepsen to AC/DC, while on the bike they embraced a similarly entertaining, attacking approach to racing.

In these early years, their strategy at the Tour de France was to target stage wins, particularly in the opening week of the race. Doing so delivered great success in their second appearance in 2013, when they not only won the team time trial and a stage with Simon Gerrans, but also held the yellow jersey for four days prior to the mountains.

As they grew as a team, so too did their ambitions, and soon they began to target the general classification at the Tour – though not through any of their large Australian contingent, but rather a pair of young British twins in Adam and Simon Yates. Both riders were among the peloton's hottest prospects, winning the white jersey in successive years between in 2016 and 2017 respectively, while also placing fourth and seventh in the yellow jersey classification. Yet a podium finish remained elusive, with a fourth-place overall from Simon in 2023 the closest they've come.

Now, the team adopts more of a hybrid approach, balancing their GC bids with stage hunting. All-rounder Michael Matthews (nicknamed 'Bling' for his fondness of jewellery) was re-signed in 2021 and sprinter Dylan Groenewegen followed the year after, and together they delivered the team three stage wins in the last four Tours. Both the Yates have now left, but in their place arrives Ben O'Connor, who is poised to be their new, and this time Australian, man for the GC.

ABOVE

A very happy Michael Matthews after winning stage 14 of the Tour de France, 2022

Ben O'Connor

One of a strong generation of Australian riders currently shining in the peloton, Ben O'Connor announced himself at the Tour de France at the end of the first week of the 2021 Tour de France with an enormous win in the Alps. Having gotten into the day's breakaway, he attacked at the bottom of the final climb, the Montée de Tignes, and rode away from everyone to win by an astonishingly large margin of over five minutes. From that stage, his Tour went from strength to strength, as he defied expectations to stay high in the overall classification and finished fourth overall. At the time he was known as a good climber, but not one who had ever challenged for GC at a Grand Tour before; this performance saw him enter cycling's elite.

As was apparent on the behind-the-scenes Netflix series *Tour de France: Unchained*, O'Connor is a man who wears his heart on his sleeve, and he appeared to suffer a crisis of confidence in the subsequent years, crashing out of the 2022 and mysteriously unable to find form in 2023. Though he skipped the Tour altogether last year, he enjoyed a stunning return to form, first placing fourth overall at the Giro d'Italia, then coming oh-so-close to winning the Vuelta a España, where he led the race for two whole weeks and only fell to second-place on the third-to-last day. This year he's signed for Jayco, and will return to the Tour with the aim of pushing for a podium finish. Despite promising much in the lead-up to both the following Tours de France, by placing on the podium at the key warm-up race, Critérium du Dauphiné, he has not managed to scale those heights since, with a crash forcing him to abandon the 2022 edition, and form mysteriously eluding him last year. But if things fall into place this year, he has the talent to again push for the podium.

ABOVE
Ben O'Connor in action at the Volta a la Comunitat Valenciana in 2025

LIDL-TREK

Back in 2011, when a new team called Leopard Trek first came into being, it seemed likely that they'd be protagonists in the race for the yellow jersey for many years to come. They formed as a vehicle for Andy and Frank Schleck, a pair of spindly-built brothers from Luxembourg who were at the time two of the best climbers in the world – a status confirmed in the Tour de France that year when, by finishing second and third respectively, they became the first siblings in the race's history to finish on the podium together.

Yet that would be as good as things got for both the brothers and the team. Though he does have a Tour de France title to his name (he was retroactively awarded the 2010 yellow jersey while riding for a different team, after the man who beat him that year, Alberto Contador, was stripped of the title for a doping offence), Andy never fully delivered on his potential, and he retired early in 2014 at the age of just 29 following three years of poor form and injury. Frank, meanwhile, never got his career back on track after a doping ban in 2012.

Without their two marquee riders, the team lacked direction. They made a habit of signing aging stars who were past their best, and received only mediocre returns – with the exception of a third-place finish from a 35-year-old Richie Porte in 2020, the team failed to crack the top five at the Tour in the years following the Schlecks' inaugural outing. In recent years they've found more success chasing stage wins, with one coming in 2021 from a breakaway by Bauke Mollema, and a couple more the following two years from sprinting all-rounder Mads Pedersen, but there has been no GC challenge.

Could that be about to change? In 2023 Lidl took over as the team's main sponsors, and though their supermarkets might specialise in budget groceries, they're prepared to splash out investing in the cycling team. They're yet to land a marquee name to target the yellow jersey, so for now the priority will continue to be stage wins, but watch this space.

Jonathan Milan

From Mario Cipollini in the 1990s to Alessandro Petacchi in the 2000s, there has been an illustrious lineage of prolific Italian sprinters in recent decades of Tour history. Could 24-year-old Jonathan Milan be their heir? Like them, he's tall, imposing, and boasts explosive speed in a sprint finish which, if delivered into position by his lead-out train, few if anyone can compete with. Milan is poised to make his Tour debut this year, having made a name for himself in both the last two editions of the Giro d'Italia, winning a stage in 2023, and three more last year. He's still a raw talent, and hasn't yet mastered a sprinting technique to make the most of the pure power he can produce, but there's no telling how high his ceiling is once he gets that right. And, unlike Cipollini and Petacchi, he's surprisingly strong on the climbs for a big man, making him more than just a pure sprinter, as proven by his successive victories in the points classification at the Giro. Now, he has his sights on the green jersey at the Tour.

RIGHT

Jonathan Milan wearing the purple jersey at the Giro d'Italia 2024

TREK
TREK
SRAM
AEOLUS
BONTRAGER
AEOLUS
Santini

MOVISTAR TEAM

Dating all the way back to 1980, no elite team in the peloton has as long a history as Team Movistar. And in that time, few can match them in terms of success at the Tour de France. Pedro Delgado won them their first yellow jersey in 1988, and he was followed by Miguel Induráin, a rider who would go on to define cycling in the early nineties. In the era of long time trials, nobody could stop Big Mig, who won his first Tour in 1991, and continued to do so, year in, year out, by seemingly even bigger margins each time. In 1995 he became one of only four riders to win five Tours, and the first to have done so in successive years.

Only one other Tour victory has come since Induráin's retirement in 1996, when Óscar Pereiro was surprisingly triumphant in 2006, but the team continued to be protagonists in the new millennium led by a new talisman in Alejandro Valverde. He might never have won the Tour, but was a reliably consistent source of major victories throughout the whole of his extraordinarily long career (save for a mid-career interruption for a doping ban), delivering countless classics, stages in all three Grand Tours and a World Championships title, before finally retiring at the end of last season aged 42.

The latter years of the Valverde era were also characterised by some dysfunctionality, however, as you can tell watching the behind-the-scenes Netflix documentary *The Least Expected Day*. As good as Valverde was, it was Nairo Quintana who represented the team's best hope of winning yellow, and the enigmatic Colombian made the podium three times between 2013 - 2016. His and Valverde's relationship always appeared strained, and the same was the case with many other big-name arrivals who briefly rode for them, and the team never made the most of the talent on their books. Things have grown less complicated in recent years now that Enric Mas has firmly established himself as their leader, but what they've gained in clarity they've lost in quality, as a team that once boasted great strength in depth now looks worryingly thin.

Enric Mas

Enric Mas lays claim to the dubious honour of being the best GC contender in the peloton never to have won a Grand Tour. He's come very close, having finished runner-up at the Vuelta a España three times in his career. And he's also one of the most dependable riders for reaching peak form at just the right time, making the top six in all but three of his last ten Grand Tour appearances since 2020. But he's lacked a certain cutting edge to make the extra step and become a Grand Tour champion.

While he continues to excel at his native Vuelta a España, finishing third overall last year, he's lost his way at the Tour de France in recent years, contracting Covid in 2022, crashing out on the opening day of the 2023 edition, and struggling for form last year. Having turned 30 in January, he's starting to run out of time to better his career-high Tour de France finish of fifth-place from 2020.

RIGHT

Enric Mas during his time trial at stage 20 of the 2021 Tour de France

ABUS
CANYON
CANYON
CANYON
CANYON

SOUDAL QUICK-STEP

Since being formed from the old Mapei team in 2003, no other team has won Tour de France stages as prolifically as Quick Step. Though they've never been especially interested in chasing after high finishes on the overall classification and, as a Belgian outfit, see the spring classics in their native Flanders as the highlight of their season, a focus on sprint wins has seen them amass over half a century of stage victories over the last two decades.

Flemish superstar Tom Boonen was responsible for many of those during the 2000s, but from 2013 the wins came more frequently as they perfected the art of the bunch sprint. What was especially impressive was how they continued to have success despite operating a revolving door of constant changes – though Mark Cavendish and Marcel Kittel each had successful stints over multiple editions, the team entered every Tour between 2017 – 2022 with a different sprinter each time, and every one of them managed at least one stage win, most of them more. These successes were built less on the individual sprinter themselves, and more on the support rides surrounding them, who were so well-trained and fine-tuned that it seemed not to matter which rider it was they were delivering to the line.

Despite having become masters of bunch sprinting, Soudal Quick-Step have dramatically changed priorities since last year. Perhaps spurred by a thrilling Tour in 2019, when they surprisingly found themselves defending the yellow jersey deep into the race courtesy of home favourite Julian Alaphilippe, for the 2023 edition they neglected to even bring a sprinter to the race, instead focusing exclusively on GC with young prodigy Remco Evenepoel. The decision was justified, as Evenepoel finished third overall, delivering the team a first Tour de France podium finish in their long history. Their 2025 Tour isn't expected to be quite so single-minded, with the prolific form of current sprinter Tim Merlier's in other races set to earn him a spot on the line-up and a chance to go for stage wins in the bunch finishes. But stages are no longer enough; now, they have their sights firmly set on the yellow jersey.

Mikel Landa

With his mournful expression and past tensions with teammates, Mikel Landa has developed a reputation for being a little temperamental. But that's unfair, as in reality he's one of the most reliable performers at the Tour de France, having only finished lower than seventh in one of his last six appearances. He is also a great team player, having helped Chris Froome to victory in 2017 while riding for Team Sky, and Richard Carapaz to win the Giro d'Italia at Movistar in 2018. This record encouraged Soudal Quick-Step to sign him up with the specific role of aiding Remco Evenepoel in the mountains, and he delivered with aplomb, providing his leader all the support he required while also managing a fifth place overall finish for himself. What is true, though, is that he has always lacked that little bit extra required for personal glory. And despite his undeniable talent for climbing, he has never won a Grand Tour.

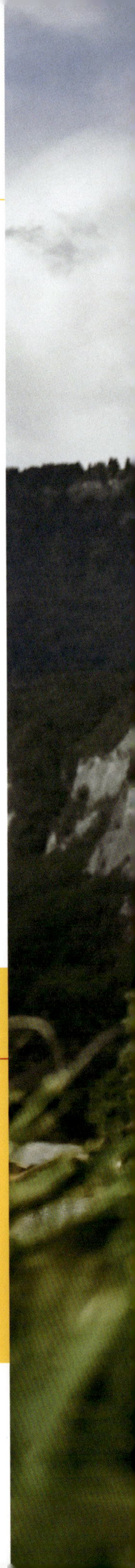

RIGHT

Julian Alaphilippe riding in the Alps during the 2023 Tour de France

SPECIALIZED
SOUDAL
NAPOLEON SPORTS
QUICK-STEP FLOORS
QUICK-STEP
S-WORKS
OUTRIDE

TEAM VISMA-LEASE A BIKE

In 2023, Visma-Lease a Bike (then known as Jumbo-Visma) reached heights no other team has managed in the history of the sport, by becoming the first to win all three of cycling's Grand Tours in the same season. This unprecedented achievement built upon their success the year before, when Jonas Vingegaard became the first rider to win the Tour de France in the team's long, 40-year history.

It took a long time for them to reach the top. In the years preceding Vingegaard's maiden success in 2022, they'd been getting closer and closer to the yellow jersey, with Steven Kruijswijk, Primož Roglič and Vingegaard each making the podium between 2019-2021 without quite claiming the top spot. Prior to that, their last brush with Tour de France glory came way back in 2007, when Michael Rasmussen spent nine days in the yellow jersey at the 2007 Tour. Although they'd always been a successful team prior to this, they were confined to doing well in the one-day classics and individual stage wins rather than for overall victories, with a roster of riders more suitable for the flat landscape of their native Netherlands than the high mountains of the Tour de France. Rasmussen therefore promised to elevate them to new heights, but the dream quickly turned into a nightmare when he was kicked off the race for a doping violation, just four days away from victory.

The fallout from this scandal, and another a few years later when accusations were made about systematic doping at the team during the 2000s forced the team to face up to some uncomfortable truths, as most of the cycling world did at this time. Longstanding sponsors Rabobank withdrew funding, and years of mediocrity followed - but crucially, it was largely scandal-free mediocrity, as the team sought to rebuild their reputation. In 2019, Mike Teunissen became the first rider from the team to wear the yellow jersey since Rasmussen after he won the opening stage, a moment which began the new, redemptive golden age the team are enjoying now. By 2020 they'd overthrown Ineos Grenadiers as the peloton's new patrons, and two years later they used their collective power to win the yellow jersey with Vingegaard. Bad luck with injuries hampered their Tour campaign in 2024, where they were unable to make it three successive overall victories in a row as UAE Team Emirates' Tadej Pogačar instead ran away with success. But they remain a formidable force and are determined to reclaim the title this year.

Sepp Kuss

Vingegaard, Roglič and Van Aert might be the marquee names who have received all of the headlines and glory during the team's recent renaissance, but Sepp Kuss deserves a special mention for his sheer selflessness. He's that rare luxury in professional cycling, an elite climber who's happy to sacrifice any personal ambition in order to ride instead as arguably the world's best super-domestique. In that role, he has played an essential role in both Vingegaard's two Tour de France victories and all three of Roglič's Vuelta a España titles for the team, where he has reliably stuck by his leaders' side when the going has gotten tough in the high mountains and all other teammates have been dropped. In 2022, the modest Coloradan enjoyed some well-deserved glory for himself at the Vuelta, when, almost by accident, he found himself in the overall lead during the first week, and defended that lead all the way to the finish to seal a surprise overall victory.

BELOW
Jumbo-Visma competing in the team time trial on stage two of the 2022 Tour de France

UAE TEAM EMIRATES

When Tadej Pogačar stunned the cycling world by winning the 2020 Tour de France, he catapulted UAE Team Emirates to a status they were not yet ready for. Suddenly this team, that had previously been also-rans in the race for yellow jersey, were the home of the Tour de France champion. If they were to defend his title and provide adequate support for Pogačar going forward, they'd need to invest and improve. Prior to Pogačar's bursting onto the scene, the team had been a middling World Tour team. A takeover by the United Arab Emirates state in 2017 had seen them hire more riders outside of the smaller Italian bubble of riders that characterised their previous incarnation as Lampre, but major results were still far from forthcoming.

When Pogačar changed all that with his triumphant ride in 2020, he did so without much need for support. As a debutant only regarded as an outside favourite, he was not put under much pressure by the other GC contenders, while only taking the yellow jersey for the final day of the race meant the team never had to carry the heavy burden of defending it. They would not be afforded the luxury of such passivity when defending the title in 2021, however, so the need to bulk up with reinforcements was clear. In came two-time King of the Mountains winner Rafał Majka, while promising young American Brandon McNulty was deployed to the Tour as a domestique, and together they helped bolster the climbing line-up. Pogačar might not have needed an awful lot of assistance as he waltzed away from everyone in the mountains, but his teammates were there when he needed them, and were a reassuring presence as they controlled the race from the moment he took yellow in the first week.

They continued to improve in the years since, adding Marc Soler in 2022 and Adam Yates in 2023 to provide yet more quality support for Pogačar in the mountains. The problem was, so did arch-rivals Visma-Lease a Bike, and the two teams have engaged in an arms race of sorts as they battle to become the Tour's strongest team. Pogačar had to settle for two consecutive second-place finishes behind their leader Jonas Vingegaard, being outmanoeuvred and isolated by him in the Alps to lose the yellow jersey in 2022, and failing to crack their robust defence with multiple attacks in 2023. But last year, with help from Tour debutants and climbing super-domestiques João Almeida and Juan Ayuso, they stormed back with a vengeance, asserting themselves as the race's dominant team and regaining the yellow jersey. This year, they're the team to beat.

João Almeida

With his hunched, rocking pedalling style and gurning facial expressions, it's hard to miss João Almeida in the peloton. Yet this belies a rider who is actually much more calculating and controlled than his appearance might suggest. He's unusual in that he rides at his own pace, paying little heed to those around him - it's common to see him drop out of the peloton at the start of a climb, only to re-emerge again before the summit and overtake the tiring riders ahead. It's an approach that has made the Portuguese rider one of the most consistent and dependable GC contenders in the peloton, demonstrated by how the only times he has failed to make the top ten in the eight Grand Tour appearances of his career have been when he's contracted Covid. And last year, on debut at the Tour de France, he produced the best performance of his career to date, finishing fourth overall while playing a role in Pogačar's overall triumph.

ABOVE

Tadej Pogačar and Slovenian compatriot and UAE Team Emirates teammate Jan Polanc embrace each other during the final stage of the 2021 Tour de France

As a race that has taken place for over a century, many traditions have grown over the years at the Tour de France. It now has its own firmly established iconography, with things like the yellow jersey, and the sight of cyclists pedalling along the Champs-Élysées recognised around the globe. These traditions all have a rich history behind them, and are a key part of what makes the Tour so special.

THE TRA

LCL
Santini
UAE
Emirates
ISRAEL
PREMIER TECH
Krys
INEOS
GRENADIER

DITIONS

THE YELLOW JERSEY

No item is as emblematic to the Tour de France, or to the whole sport of cycling, as the yellow jersey. The prize awarded to the winner of the overall classification, it's one of the most instantly recognisable sights in sport. Even someone who knows next to nothing about cycling will likely know it, and every professional dreams of wearing it.

Although not awarded in the very early era of the Tour de France, it still has a very long history, having first been introduced in the 1919 edition. It's become so familiar that the question rarely comes to mind, but: why yellow? It's hardly an obvious choice, compared with, say, gold, given its sporting associations with glory and success. Well, the idea was for a bright eye-catching colour that would stick out in the peloton. And, unsurprisingly for a sport in which sponsorship has always been so integral, there were reasons related to advertisement, too – the newspaper *L'Auto*, which organised the race, was coloured yellow.

Such is the prestige of the jersey that even wearing it for one day is considered a huge achievement. It's a common sight to see a rider moved to tears when being handed it on the podium. Many riders target the opening few stages of the Tour with the primary intention of getting to wear it, even if they have no chance of keeping it all the way to Paris.

Unsurprisingly, Eddy Merckx has worn the jersey more than anyone else, as befitting his status as the greatest cyclist of all time. In terms of total number of yellow jerseys won (ie, number of Tours de France won, not just days spent leading it), he's tied with three other riders: Jacques Anquetil, Bernard Hinault and Miguel Induráin. Each of these greats have won it five times, which seems to be the limit that no-one is able to surpass. Lance Armstrong did break the record by winning it seven times during his career, but those results have all since been retrospectively annulled due to revelations about his systematic doping.

Chris Froome

In the last few decades, nobody has been more synonymous with the yellow jersey than Chris Froome. He won the Tour de France four times between 2013 and 2017, falling just short of equalling the all-time record, and in that time has worn the jersey 59 times. Each year, he followed pretty much the same pattern, taking the yellow jersey towards the end of the first week, then defending it all the way to Paris. Once he took control of it, it was almost impossible for anyone to take it off him – in fact, only once did he concede it, and even that occasion was only for two days.

Holding yellow that much means a lot of press conferences and media obligations, therefore we've gotten to know Froome well over the years as a polite, softly spoken, calm man, with exactly the kind of level-headed temperament you'd expect of someone so apt at handling pressure. Following years of injuries, fitness problems, and simply getting old, the 39-year-old is well past his best and no longer capable of challenging for yellow, but would like to return to the Tour one last time before he retires.

BELOW
Chris Froome wearing the yellow jersey in front of Romain Bardet during stage 18 of the 2017 Tour de France

DOIMO
LIQUIGAS
cannondale
SUGOi
PMU
lotto
ristora
RUDY

THE GREEN JERSEY

The yellow jersey might be the most famous item of clothing in cycling, but for many riders at the Tour de France, it's the green jersey they dream of wearing. Unlike the overall classification, which is based around the time it takes to finish the race, the green jersey is a points-based competition (also known as the 'points classification'), in which points are awarded to the highest place finishes on every stage (with bonuses available at intermediate sprints). The winner is the rider who finishes the Tour with the greatest number of points accumulated.

Consequently, the green jersey suits a very different type of rider than those who target the yellow jersey - rather than the climbers who compete for overall victory, it's the sprinters who feature in the bunch finishes that contest this classification. The system is geared towards sprinters, too, considering that the most common type of stage are flat ones that end in bunch sprints, and that more points are awarded on these stages compared with the climber-friendly mountain stages.

However, the 'sprinter's jersey' label that has been assigned to the points classification doesn't quite tell the whole story. Winning it isn't simply a matter of being the fastest sprinter at the race - in fact, on only three occasions since 2008 has the winner of the green jersey also won more pure sprints than any other sprinter. Instead, it's all-rounders who can consistently pick up points in the bunch finishes in amongst the pure sprinters, and then forge ahead by using their other attributes to add to their tally in stages with more complicated terrain, who usually succeed. The history of green jersey winners is, therefore, made up mostly of dynamic, exciting all-rounders who have much more strings to their bow than just fast sprint. Mark Cavendish is unquestionably the greatest sprinter of his generation, but has only won the green jersey twice, with more versatile riders like Peter Sagan and Thor Hushovd defeating him over the years. Further back, Mario Cipollini was the fastest man of the 1990s, but never won the green jersey, while his rival Erik Zabel triumphed in six consecutive years.

Zabel broke the record that has since been broken by Sagan, and was formerly held by Irishman Sean Kelly, who perhaps epitomises better than anybody the archetypal all-rounder capable of doing everything. By winning it four times, he surpassed the previous highest total of three jointly held by Jan Janssen, Freddy Maertens and Eddy Merckx, at a time when the green jersey competition was less specialised, and had more overlap with the overall contenders.

Peter Sagan

Since the points classification was first introduced in 1953, no rider has won more than Peter Sagan's seven titles. He was untouchable during the 2010s, during which time he used his unparalleled consistency, fast sprint, climbing ability and uncanny knack for always positioning himself well and never crashing to ensure that nobody even came close to beating him. With his cheeky charisma and crowd-pleasing showmanship, he became arguably the biggest star of the sport, before retiring at the end of last year following a few leaner seasons since his last green jersey title in 2019.

LEFT
Peter Sagan does the 'running man' celebration upon crossing the line to win stage three of the 2012 Tour de France

THE KING OF THE MOUNTAINS

Watch any stage of the Tour de France, and among the thousands of spectators lining the roadside you'll see many decked out in polka-dot paraphernalia, with accessories ranging from cycling caps to tote bags, all decorated with the same red and white colours. It's all linked to the polka-dot jersey, the prize given to the macho-sounding King of the Mountains classification, which is, aside from the yellow jersey, the most synonymous with the Tour de France.

Points are awarded to the first few riders to reach the summit of each classified climb, and the harder the climb, the more points are on offer. It is therefore historically a prize associated with the pure climbers, and its early winners include legendary names from the early years of the sport like Fausto Coppi, Charly Gaul, and in particular Federico Bahamontes, the so-called 'Eagle of Toledo' who won the classification six times. Neither he or any of these riders ever actually wore the iconic jersey, however, as it wasn't introduced until the 1975 edition, when Lucian Van Impe won it. The Belgian went on to become the man most associated with it, and equalled Bahamontes' record by winning it six times himself. Both he and Bahamontes weren't good enough all-round to win the yellow jersey more than once each, but in the mountains, they were indomitable.

In the 1990s and 2000s, the nature of the competition changed. Rather than being won by the best climber among the GC contenders, riders would triumph by getting into the right breakaways with the specific target of acquiring points without competing head-to-head against the yellow jersey candidates. Richard Virenque perfected this approach, and in 2004 surpassed both Bahamontes and Van Impe to take his seventh title, a record that stands until today. However, few believe he is as great a climber as those riders, but rather someone who smartly gamed the system.

Although riders still had to be great climbers in order to win the polka-dot jersey with this approach, with the likes of Nairo Quintana, Rafał Majka and Julian Alaphilippe all triumphing over the past decade, it did take the lustre off the competition. So in order to avert this trend and swing the advantage back towards the very best climbers, the organisers changed the rules in order to place more emphasis on the mountains more significant to the yellow jersey race. This did initially have the unwanted effect of the top GC contenders winning the classification by default without even targeting it at all – as was the case between 2020-2022, where the polka-dot jersey winner has been the same as the yellow jersey winner. But the last couple of years have seen a welcome resurgence of entertaining, non-GC climbing specialists taking the jersey, with Italian Giulio Ciccone triumphing in 2023, and Richard Carapaz doing so last year.

Richard Virenque

Richard Virenque had this competition all figured out in the 1990s, regularly beating superior climbers like Marco Pantani through his canny exploitation of the rules to efficiently accumulate points, and won it four times in a row between 1994-1997. He was caught up in the controversy of the Festina Affair in 1998, but didn't admit to doping until a few years later – and even then only partially, saying he did so "willingly, but without knowing". Despite the scandal, he remained popular among the French public, and returned to ultimately win a seventh King of the Mountains title, which remains the record to this day.

BELOW

Richard Virenque wearing the polka-dot jersey during stage 15 of the 2004 Tour de France

THE WHITE JERSEY

Awarded since 1975 as the prize for the best young rider at the Tour de France, the white jersey has become one of the four top prizes at the race. It operates on the same principle as the yellow jersey in that the rider who completes the Tour in the least amount of time wins, but only riders young enough (specifically, those aged less than 26-year-old on January 1st of the year of that race) are eligible.

Sometimes, the same rider who wins yellow also wins white: Laurent Fignon, Jan Ullrich, Alberto Contador, Andy Schleck, Egan Bernal all managed this, while in 2021 Tadej Pogačar became the first rider to do so twice. This has become especially common in recent editions, as the average age of the top contenders has decreased, leading to some calls to reduce the eligible age for the white jersey.

More often though, winning the white jersey is a sign of youthful potential and promise of future, greater success at the Tour. Greg LeMond and Marco Pantani both went on to win the yellow jersey after first winning white, while Ullrich and Schleck's yellow jersey/white jersey double came after they'd already previously won white. With a total of three white jersey titles each, Ullrich and Schleck had also held the record for having won the most, until Pogačar broke that record by adding a fourth title in 2023.

A PRECURSOR TO SUCCESS?

Although winning it is seen as having a bright future ahead of you, a look back at the history of the white jersey suggests that it's difficult to maintain success enjoyed early on in a Tour de France career. Jan Ullrich looked all set to be a sensation when he became the first man to win the classification three times, but never again managed to win the yellow jersey after he turned 26, finding himself unable to get the better of Lance Armstrong. Other multiple-winners of the jersey since have found their careers fizzle out as they've gotten older; Andy Schleck retired just four years after his third time winning it, while Colombian Nairo Quintana has still never bettered the performances that saw him win the jersey in 2013 and 2015. Last year's winner Remco Evenepoel will hope the same fate does not befall him.

RIGHT

Tadej Pogačar descends the Col de la Madeleine while in the white jersey during stage 17 of the 2020 Tour de France

MET
UAE
Krys Krys
LE COQ SPORT
Krys
Emirates
COLNAGO
COLNAGO

THE GRAND DÉPART

Translating into English as the 'great departure', the Grand Départ is the name given to the opening stage of each Tour de France. It's where the party gets going, and anticipation builds and builds in whichever town is hosting it, before huge crowds take to the streets to watch on the day of the big event. These days it changes location each year, as towns from France and all across Europe compete for the honour of being selected to host the biggest cycling event of the year.

In the early years of the Tour, the Grand Départ was always held in Paris, with just one single exception (1926, Évian) before 1951. But from that year onwards the location would vary each time, including a first ever foreign Grand Départ in Amsterdam in 1954. In the 1970s these foreign ventures became more common, and since the new millennia as many Grand Départs have been held abroad as they have in France. While that might appear to go against the logic of a race called the 'Tour of France', these cross-border excursions always make for a special occasion, as passionate fans and curious locals alike flock to the roadside in their thousands to enjoy the novelty of seeing the Tour visit.

Great Britain has hosted the Grand Départ twice, first in London for the 2007 race, then Yorkshire for 2014, while Ireland welcomed the Tour earlier in 1998. Tuscany became the first ever Italian location to have the honour last year, and this year the race will set off from France for the first time in four years, with a start in the northern town of Lille.

YORKSHIRE 2014

Nobody who was in Yorkshire to greet the Tour de France in 2014 will ever forget the experience. During a time of great success for British cycling, an enthusiastic public turned up in stunningly high numbers, crowding the host towns of Leeds, Harrogate, York and Sheffield as well as the picturesque countryside in between. The hilly terrain of Yorkshire also made a great theatre for racing, where eccentrically named climbs, such as the Côte de Blubberhouses, produced thrilling, attacking racing, with the eventual overall winner Vincenzo Nibali winning the second stage with a surprise attack. A crash on the finishing straight might have prevented home favourite Mark Cavendish from potentially winning the opening stage (instead, German sprinter Marcel Kittel was victorious), but the support of the crowd still led many to call it the greatest Grand Départ ever, and its popularity spawned a new Tour de Yorkshire stage race that was held each year until 2019.

RIGHT

Fans flock to the roadside to watch the Tour de France pass through Yorkshire, during the opening stage of the 2014 Tour de France

THE CHAMPS-ÉLYSÉES FINALE

Normally populated by tourists, shoppers and cars, for one day of the year the Champs-Élysées boulevard in central Paris becomes a paradise of cycling. With the sole exception of last year, when it was moved to Nice to accommodate the Paris Olympics, every Tour de France since 1975 has finished here, in which time it has become one of the race's most famous traditions. Taking in all the familiar tourist sites, from the Arc de Triomphe and the Louvre to the Eiffel Tower, the stage functions as a showcase and advertisement of Paris. And the riders themselves enjoy something of a holiday, as the custom is for a premature truce to be called in the general classification race, which is tacitly agreed to have come to a conclusion the day before. Therefore there's a unique, end-of-term feel to this first half of this climactic stage as they approach Paris from one of the outskirt towns, with riders able to laugh and joke together and even share a glass of champagne in celebration of having made it to the end of one of sport's most gruelling endeavours.

But although the race for the yellow jersey is considered over, there is still a stage win up for grabs - and not just any stage, but one that's known as the unofficial 'sprinter's world championships' for its importance to the fast finishes. For them, this isn't just the most prestigious Tour de France stage to win, but the most prestigious sprint of the whole season, and most of the truly great sprinters of the recent decades have won here, with Mark Cavendish, André Greipel, Marcel Kittel, Robbie McEwen and Djamolidine Abdoujaparov all winning on multiple occasions at the height of their powers.

Every edition of this stage has ended in a sprint since 2006, but that might change this year as the organisers have altered the route by interrupting the otherwise flat terrain to add three ascents up to Montmartre, the same cobbled hill that featured during the Olympics road race in 2024. One of the Tour's longest traditions could therefore be about to change. On only seven occasions has the stage not been won in a sprint, and only four times since the end of the 1970s. One of those occasions, in 1989, was one of the most memorable in Tour history. For one year only the Champs-Élysées held a time trial rather than the usual sprinters' road stage, and the results were hugely dramatic as Greg LeMond usurped Laurent Fignon to win the yellow jersey by just eight seconds - a winning margin that remains the smallest in Tour history, in an edition that many believe to be the greatest ever.

Mark Cavendish

Unsurprisingly given his status as the best sprinter of all-time, Manxman Mark Cavendish holds the record of four stage wins on the Champs-Élysées. These were achieved in successive years between 2009 - 2012, during which time he was virtually untouchable in the Tour de France sprints. A stunning comeback in 2021 from long-term injury problems saw him add another four stage wins to his overall career tally, which pulled him level with Eddy Merckx on the all-time leaderboard for most ever Tour de France stage wins with 34, and last year he memorably became the outright record holder with a 35th career win.

RIGHT
The peloton race on the Champs-Élysées, with the Arc de Triomphe in the background

THE MO

The mighty mountains of the Alps and the Pyrenees are the stages on which the great stories of the Tour de France are played out. Their stunning scenery intimidates and strikes fear into even the most hardened cyclist, and their huge size provide the great test that makes the Tour de France such a brutal challenge. Over the years particular climbs have gained legendary status, witnessing countless stories in Tour history.

INTAINS

ALPE D'HUEZ

Alpe d'Huez is the Tour de France at its most populist. It's not the connoisseur's favourite climb, and isn't actually as hard as the race's other legendary mountains, yet its fame nevertheless transcends them all. Every time that it's included in the Tour, crowds unrivalled in size flock to its slopes, partly for the sporting spectacle of seeing the race go by, but also to take part in the biggest party in cycling, that starts many days in advance as visitors set up camp early. There's always a rowdy, drunken atmosphere by the time the riders arrive, which sometimes can get out of hand, as happened in 1999, when Italian Giuseppe Guerini nearly missed out on a stage win after colliding with an overzealous fan trying to take a picture.

So what makes this particular mountain such a fan favourite? The layout of the climb is significant, as the way its infamous 21 hairpin bends compress the action and turn it into a natural, spectator-friendly theatre to watch the race. Each one of these bends also commemorates former stage winners on the climb, and the illustrious list of names included adds to the climb's mystique as a venue where legends are made. It helps also that the climb has always been used at the end of a stage rather than in the middle, as it is therefore always crucial in the race for overall victory. Received wisdom has it that if you can make it to the top of Alpe d'Huez as leader of the Tour, then you more often than not win yellow in Paris.

The great Italian Fausto Coppi was the first ever winner here in 1952 back when such a mountain top finish was still a novelty, but only after its return in 1976 did it become a regular Tour fixture, and rarely since have more than two years passed without a visit. Dutch riders were especially successful on the climb during the 1970s and '80s, with Joop Zoetemelk and Hennie Kuiper contributing to eight wins for the nation. The climb has since become known as the Dutch Mountain, and their orange-clad fans lead the party on the famously noisy 'Dutch Corner', although supporters from other nations such as Norway have rivalled them more recently.

Ascents in the 1990s and 2000s became quicker as the likes of Marco Pantani and Lance Armstrong won stages in an era blighted by the widespread use of performance enhancing drugs. Thankfully recent years have seen rides just as epic but without the controversy, with particular success from British riders - in 2018 Geraint Thomas became the first ever rider to win here while wearing the yellow jersey, and in 2022 Tom Pidcock took victory to announce himself as a major climbing talent.

INTRA-TEAM TENSION AT THE 1986 TOUR

The 1986 Tour de France is infamous for the tension and rivalry between defending champion Bernard Hinault and his younger teammate Greg LeMond, but on Alpe d'Huez a truce prevented things from getting out of hand. Despite vowing to work as a domestique for LeMond, Hinault had attacked throughout the Tour, and had done so again on the climbs preceding Alpe d'Huez so that the two were away together from the rest of the field. The stage seemed set for yet more attacks from Hinault on the climb, especially with the partisan crowds cheering on their French favourite. But none was forthcoming, and the two instead worked together and ultimately linked arms as they crossed the finish line to ensure LeMond won the yellow jersey - even if Hinault did appear to nudge his wheel forward a fraction to be the official stage winner.

BELOW

Tom Pidcock climbs through a crowded 'Dutch corner' of Alpe d'Huez during stage 12 of the 2022 Tour de France, on his way to victory

COL D'AUBISQUE

"Assassins!" That was the accusatory cry directed to the Tour de France organisers by Octave Lapize, upon being one of the first riders to reach the summit of the Col d'Aubisque on its first inclusion in the race in 1910. It was one of four Pyrenean mountains tackled that day that has since become known as the 'Circle of Death', a watershed moment in Tour history in which the high mountains first became a part of its essence.

Despite the initial hostility from Lapize and others, all of the climbs used for that stage have become common features of the Tour, with the Aubisque now having been visited the second most times of any mountain after its neighbour and fellow Circle of Death member, the Col du Tourmalet. The Aubisque may not be quite as monstrous as that mighty mountain, but it's still a huge, lengthy obstacle, whether tackled from its more direct, steeper side via Laruns, or the longer and more uneven direction that first reaches the Col du Soulor summit.

It's usually used as a mountain pass climbed earlier in a stage, but the few times it has functioned as a summit finish has seen plenty of drama. In 1985, Stephen Roche defied fashion conventions by donning a one-piece skinsuit usually used only in time trials, the kind of thing that was very much a faux pas back then, but paved the way for modern cycling's embracing of technically advanced clothing. His choice was justified, as he treated the short, 52km stage like a time trial by attacking early on the Aubisque and soloing for victory. In 2007, Michael Rasmussen and Alberto Contador engaged in another mano y mano, stop/start attacking duel that had waged all Tour, with Rasmussen coming out on top in the yellow jersey to win the stage. It looked as though he'd all but sealed overall victory, but was kicked off the race just hours later for lying about his whereabouts to the doping authorities earlier in the year. Contador went on to win the Tour instead.

A TREACHEROUS DESCENT

The ascent of the Aubisque might be the hardest part physically, but its descent is the most dangerous. In 1951, Dutchman Wim van Est suffered a scare when he fell into a ravine on the way down, having descended the mountain recklessly in a desperate attempt to defend the yellow jersey that was under threat after he'd lost ground on the climb. The story that he fell a whole 70 metres might be exaggerated, but what is true is that he was helped back up via an improvised tow rope fashioned together with plaited bike tyres. "Here on 17 July 1951 the cyclist Wim van Est fell 70 metres" read s a monument that now marks the spot on the mountain. "He survived but lost the yellow jersey."

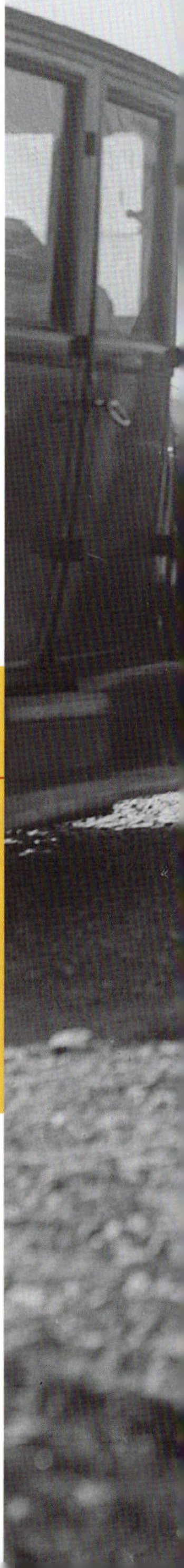

RIGHT
Arriving at the summit of the Col d'Aubisque, during stage 9 of the 1929 Tour de France

COL DU GALIBIER

Near the top of the Col du Galibier is a monument to Henri Desgrange, the original organiser of the Tour de France. It was his dream to send the riders up this enormous climb, and, after the experiment of visiting the Pyrenees the year before, did so for the 1911 Tour de France. Only three men made it to the summit without walking, among them the first to reach it, Émile Georget, and just as had happened the previous year, the competitors berated Desgrange for expecting them to ride up it. But he was smitten, declaring it the great climb of the Tour de France, against which the previous year's Circle of Death cols paled in comparison. It's been a regular fixture of the race ever since.

What makes the Galibier such an intimidating climb is just how high into the heavens it rises. Its summit stands at 2,642 metres above sea level, at which height the air becomes thin and difficult to breathe. Add to that the increasingly difficult gradient, and the barren nature of the treeless landscape, and the final kilometres of this monster are truly horrible. It's regularly the highest point of the whole Tour de France (for which the 'Souvenir Henri Desgrange' prize is awarded to whichever rider reaches the top first) and when in 2011 it hosted a stage finish for the first and only time, it became the highest summit finish in Tour history.

It's usually used earlier in the stage, often prior to a finish at another mountain such as Alpe d'Huez, and therefore few are brave enough to attack so early. But the greats have left their mark on the climb nonetheless, from Italians Fausto Coppi and Gino Bartali duelling in the snow in 1952, to Marco Pantani's long-range solo attack to take yellow en route to overall victory in 1998, while contemporary legend Tadej Pogačar last year dropped everybody with an explosive attack a kilometre from the top to win the first of his six stages.

THE 2011 TOUR TURNS ON ITS HEAD

To celebrate the hundredth anniversary since the climb's debut, the 2011 Tour de France featured two ascents of the Galibier, and each proved thrilling in the tight race for the yellow jersey that year. On stage 18, Andy Schleck reached the foot of the climb ahead of his rivals having boldly attacked 60km from the finish, and reached the top alone to take an epic stage victory, while behind him French underdog hero Thomas Voeckler went through a world of pain to cling on to the yellow jersey, his gurning face a pure expression of pain and suffering.

Voeckler would lose the yellow he had held so implausibly deep into the race the next day, however, when he lost ground to Schleck and Alberto Contador on the Galibier following another early attack. But the eventual winner of yellow was to be Australian Cadel Evans, who gained back enough time in the final time trial to depose Schleck from the top of the general classification.

RIGHT
The peloton takes on the Col du Galibier during stage 16 of the 2006 Tour de France

COL D'IZOARD

The Col d'Izoard may not reach quite as high into the sky as its fellow Alpine giant the Col du Galibier, but something about it is stranger and more unnerving. A lot has to do with just how remote it is, and how otherworldly the landscape towards the top is. Little grows up here, and there's barely any vegetation to break up the murky colours save for the occasional pine tree, while the rock formations jut out in imposing shapes. The striking backdrop of the Casse Déserte a few kilometres from the top, with its mess of debris and sharp grey slopes, is particularly barren, and looks like the kind of place you'd film a sci-fi picture set in an especially lonely corner of outer space.

It's not visited quite as prolifically by the Tour as it used to be, with ten appearances since 1977, but before then it was an almost annual feature following its introduction in 1922. As such, its most famous incidents have involved the greats of yore, immortalised in black and white photography rather than television pictures. Famously, Italian legends Gino Bartali and Fausto Coppi have each left their mark here. Bartali was the first to the top in both 1938 and 1948 en route to winning both his career Tour de France titles, but the following year met his match in the younger, cooler Coppi. Coppi generously waited for Bartali after he punctured on the descent, and allowed him to take the stage victory on what was his 35th birthday, but Coppi would take the yellow jersey from him the very next day and dethrone him as Tour champion in a symbolic changing of the guard. There's now a monument to Coppi near the top, where his face is depicted in silhouette, alongside another of Louison Bobet, the first ever French rider to win the Tour three times. No rider has ever matched Bobet's total of leading the race over its summit three times, and on each occasion he also took the stage win too.

Others like Federico Bahamontes and Eddy Merckx followed in his footsteps, until the Tour took a decade-long break away from the Col d'Izoard following the 1976 edition. But it has become popular once again in the years since, and in 2017 Frenchman Warren Barguil was victorious on the first ever summit finish on the climb, adorned in the polka-dot jersey as King of the Mountains. There's plenty of history yet to be written on this famous summit.

BARTALI'S HISTORIC RIDE

The day before climbing the Col d'Izoard at the 1948 Tour de France, Gino Bartali received a phone call from Italy's recently elected prime minister, Alcide De Gasperi. The nation had just been plunged into chaos following the assassination of communist party leader Palmiro Togliatti, and De Gasperi urged Bartali to mellow the mood of the nation. It was a lot to ask, but seemed to inspire Bartali, who embarked on a huge solo attack in the freezing rain and flew up the Izoard like a man possessed. He not only took the stage victory, but gained 18 of the 21 minutes he needed out of leader Louison Bobet to set himself up for the second yellow jersey of his career.

RIGHT
Wearing the polka-dot jersey, Warren Barguil celebrates winning stage 18 of the 2017 Tour de France, atop the Col d'Izoard

Sunweb

COL DU TOURMALET

Since its debut at the 1910 edition, no mountain has featured more at the Tour de France than the Col du Tourmalet. In that time its reputation has grown and grown as stories have accumulated about the hazards of the most feared of the Pyrenean Circle of Death, and it's become steeped in mythic folklore. The story goes that journalist Alphonse Steinès, eager for his colleague Henri Desgrange to include the Tourmalet in the Tour, defied warnings of bandits and wild bears to attempt to drive to its summit and prove its feasibility. He had to abandon his car before the top because of the snow, and was found dazed and lost by a search party in the dead of the night. Nevertheless, a – to say the least – misleading telegram sent by him announcing the climb as 'perfectly passable' was enough to persuade Desgrange, and the rest is history.

An artful statue named 'The Tourmalet Giant' now stands near the top, honouring Octave Lapize, the first rider to reach the top in 1910. Its general outline, and open mouth gasping for air, seems more designed to honour all cyclists rather than a specific individual, celebrating cycling's democratic appeal as something anyone can try if brave enough. But of all the pros and amateurs to have attempted the Tourmalet over the years, it is fittingly the greatest of all time who has produced probably the greatest ride – Eddy Merckx, who in 1969, despite already wearing the yellow jersey with a comfortable advantage, went the extra mile by attacking on the Tourmalet despite it being over 100km from the finish, and going on to win the stage by a huge margin. The myth of Merckx as an insatiable 'Cannibal' was born that day.

Stories abound before and after that ride. In 1913, the ever-unfortunate Eugène Christophe diligently followed the rules by walking many miles down the mountain to a local blacksmith in order to fix his bike broken on the descent, only to be penalised anyway for enlisting the help of a boy while repairing it. And in 2019 Thibaut Pinot and Julian Alaphilippe set French hearts racing by finishing first and second on a summit finish, raising hopes that one could win the yellow jersey, only to both fade away in the final week.

HISTORIC SUMMIT FINISH

To commemorate the climb's one hundredth anniversary, the 2010 edition of the Tour included a rare summit finish on the Tourmalet for the last mountain stage of the race, and provided the hoped-for drama with a climactic showdown for the yellow jersey between defending champion Alberto Contador and his rival Andy Schleck. Schleck was a mere eight seconds behind Contador going into the stage, but, despite multiple micro-accelerations up the mountain in misty, dreary conditions, he was unable to drop him. Nevertheless, Schleck is now recognised as the official winner of that Tour, after Contador was retrospectively disqualified for a doping offence.

RIGHT

Egan Bernal descends the Col du Tourmalet ahead of Chris Froome in the peloton during stage 19 of the 2018 Tour de France

HAUTACAM

Unfortunately, the history of cycling has been tarnished by doping and performance enhancing drugs, especially in the 1990s and 2000s, and perhaps no single mountain is now so associated with unbelievable performances that have since indeed been proven to be too good to be true than the Hautacam. Its second appearance in 1996 is infamous for being the time when Bjarne Riis, despite the hot weather and harsh gradients, flew up the mountain with apparent ease and demolished the opposition, leaving even Miguel Induráin in his wake, who on this same climb two years earlier had defended the yellow jersey with ease. It was a startling performance from a 32-year-old who had never before seemed a natural climber, and eleven years later after much speculation, he admitted that he had been aided by performance enhancing drugs.

This performance was a showcase of the kind of transformative power the EPO drug in particular had, and the next visits to the Hautacam demonstrated the influence it continued to have in the following years. In 2000, Lance Armstrong – using a similar cocktail of drugs to Riis before him – laid the foundation for his second Tour de France victory by dropping and powering away from all of his rivals, ending the day with a huge lead of over four minutes over nearest rival Jan Ullrich on GC. All of his titles would later be rescinded. Then in 2008, while cycling was beginning to seriously clean up its act, the Saunier Duval-Scott team produced a suspicious looking performance in which Leonardo Piepoli and Juan José Cobo rode away from the field to place first and second. Piepoli was later stripped of the victory for doping.

Thankfully, the two subsequent visits to the Hautacam have not been tarnished this way, as the sport of cycling redeemed itself and slowly earned the fans' trust again. Vincenzo Nibali claimed the last of his four stage wins during his all-conquering overall victory at the 2014 Tour de France on the mountain, with a ride that has, unlike those before him, stood the test of time. And just last year, it was the site of one of Tadej Pogačar and Jonas Vingegaard's many duels, and great moments of sportsmanship. On a hectic descent leading to the climb, both riders endured hairy moments, with Pogačar even falling off at one point. Vingegaard sportingly waited for his rival, and upon catching up again Pogačar exchanged a friendly handshake with him. Vingegaard showed no such mercy once they reached the Hautacam, though, dropping his rival a few kilometres from the top to take the stage and all but seal overall victory. It was a great battle, and one that could be resumed again this year when the climb hosts the finish of stage twelve.

NIBALI PROVES A POINT

While Vincenzo Nibali was leading the Tour de France in 2014, there were some who questioned the validity of his success given the absence of fellow pre-race favourites Chris Froome and Alberto Contador, both of whom had crashed out. As if on a mission to prove his worthiness, Nibali attacked early on the Hautacam during stage 18, and soloed almost 10km to the top to achieve his fourth stage win of the race. That increased his overall winning margin to over seven minutes (which remains the biggest at the Tour de France in the last quarter of a century), a victory comprehensive enough to suggest that nobody, not even the acclaimed absentees, could have stopped him.

BELOW

Jonas Vingegaard climbing the Hautacam in the yellow jersey during stage 18 of the 2022 Tour de France, en route to victory

MONT VENTOUX

'The Giant of Provence'; 'The Bald Mountain.' Mont Ventoux is such an evocative entity that it has inspired not one but two nicknames that have stuck over the years. The first alludes not only to its 'giant' size, but also its strange geographical location in the far western tip of the Alps. It's at the extreme western end of the Alps, standing alone from the rest of the mountain range so that it can be seen from many miles away from all directions. The latter describes its uniquely disquieting appearance, specifically the summit, which, with its lunar appearance, is like no other mountain climbed at the Tour de France. In contrast to the forests that characterise its lower slopes, no vegetation grows here, which is instead a desolate wilderness of dull, light grey limestone that strikes fear into the hearts of even the toughest cyclists.

Worse still, the weather up here can manifest in all kinds of different extremes, to impose yet more misery on whoever dares to try and climb to the top. Either it can reach searingly hot temperatures that risk dehydration and even heatstroke, or ludicrously blustery conditions if the mistral wind is blowing strongly from the south. Either way, added to the thinness of the air that is so hard to gasp in, this a climb that tests so much more than just the legs, and the final slog up to the seemingly always just out of reach meteorological observatory tower at the summit is perhaps the most agonising in cycling.

It's a mountain so challenging that it reduced even the great Eddy Merckx to a whimpering wreck in 1970, when he required oxygen after reaching the summit. His effort was still enough for him to win the stage en route to his second overall victory, however, and indeed Mont Ventoux has been conquered by many of the great climbers over the years. The legendary Charly Gaul won here during his only career yellow jersey win in 1958, as did Marco Pantani in 2000 - although, much to the proud Italian's fury, he only triumphed after Lance Armstrong decided to gift him the stage win by not contesting the sprint. Most recently, Chris Froome produced arguably the most powerful attack of his career to take victory during his unstoppable first overall victory in 2013, and returned three years later in bizarre circumstances when, temporarily stranded without a working bike after a collision with a television motorbike, he for a short stretch jogged up the mountain. Just about anything can happen on this mountain, so expect more drama when the Tour returns here for the first time since 2016 next year.

TRAGEDY AT THE TOUR

Mont Ventoux is haunted by the memory of Tom Simpson, one of the greatest riders of his generation who died climbing it during the 1967 Tour de France at the age of just 29. Suffering from heat exhaustion, the charismatic Brit became increasingly delirious as he neared the summit, and fell off his bike. Ignoring the pleas of his team's staff, he insisted upon getting back onto his bike, but collapsed shortly after, this time fatally. After a post-mortem confirmed traces of amphetamines in his body, the incident has since become perceived as a cautionary tale of the sport's history of drug taking, as well as its most harrowing tragedy.

BELOW
Riders pass under the observatory tower at the top of Mont Ventoux during stage 20 of the 2009 Tour de France

PUY-DE-DÔME

One of the great cycling battlegrounds of old resides neither in the Alps nor the Pyrenees, but rather the Massif Central, the vast area of highlands that covers much of south-central France. Though this region may not have the same mythical folklore of those two grander mountain ranges, the Puy-de-Dôme certainly has, and was once among the most anticipated of all the climbs of the Tour de France. As a dormant volcano it is a striking location, and though not especially long, the steepness of the gradient has made it perfect for slow motion duels between contenders at their very limit.

Many of the greats of yore have won here, from Fausto Coppi on the Tour's first visit in 1952 to Federico Bahamontes in a time trial that finished here in 1959, during the sole yellow jersey victory of his career. Above all though, it's the battle between the infamous rivals Jacques Anquetil and Raymond Poulidor in 1964 that cemented the climb's mythic status. As captured by the then-novel live television cameras, the pair rode side-by-side for much of the climb, with Poulidor claiming the stage win with a late attack, but not gaining enough time to prise the yellow jersey from his rival. Whether or not it's true that Anquetil rode beside rather than behind Poulidor in order to feign strength he didn't have and thus discourage him from attacking, what is true is that Anquetil exercised a certain psychological hold on his rival, and came out on top in all of their battles for overall glory at the Tour.

Eleven years later, another of the Tour's multiple yellow jersey winners came under immense pressure on the Puy-de-Dôme, and in this case he did not prevail. Eddy Merckx's travails were more a matter of unfortunate victimhood than lack of legs, however, as he lost time after being punched in the kidney by a spectator near the summit. Bruised and nauseous, he battled on to the top and managed to defend the yellow jersey, but not for much longer – still suffering the after-effects of the assault, he lost it to Bernard Thévenet a few days later. That turned out to be the last time he ever wore the yellow jersey.

Logistical problems related to its narrow roads and the construction of rail-track next to it prevented the Tour from visiting the Puy-de-Dôme after 1988, until 2023, when amiable Canadian Michael Woods won the stage, while modern day legends Jonas Vingegaard and Tadej Pogačar followed in the footsteps of their forebears to do battle on its slopes.

LUIS OCAÑA AND JOOP ZOETEMELK

Two riders have won twice on the Puy-de-Dôme: Luis Ocaña and Joop Zoetemelk. For Ocaña, the climb was a stage for him to emerge out of the shadow of his great rival Eddy Merckx, and prove himself a cycling great on his own terms; in 1971 he attacked the Belgian here to win the stage, and he won here again in 1973 while in the yellow jersey, just days before sealing overall victory. Zoetemelk was another rider who often found himself cast in Merckx's shadow, and in his absence, won stages at the Puy-de-Dôme in 1976 and 1978. But on both occasions he still had to settle for second place on the overall classification, first to Lucien Van Impe, and then his new foe, a young Bernard Hinault.

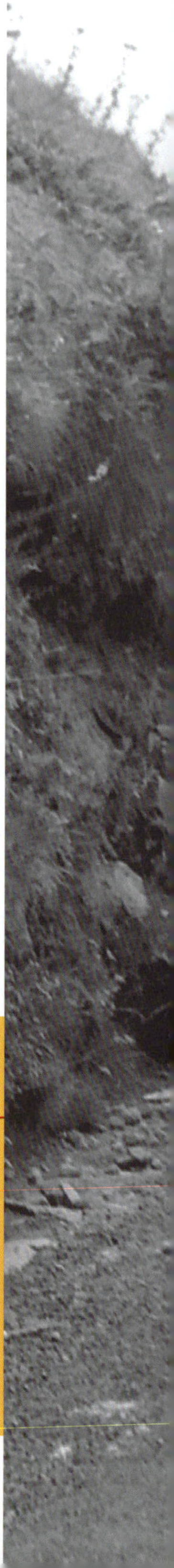

BELOW

Jacques Anquetil, left, and Raymond Poulidor duel on the Puy-de-Dôme, during the 1964 Tour de France

THE HI

From its evolution from a gimmicky publicity stunt in 1903 to the biggest annual sporting event in the world, the Tour has changed immeasurably. It's reflected everything from social changes to technological advancement, as well as the gradual professionalisation of the sport. Each era has had its stars, especially the four greats that have attained the still-unsurpassed total of five overall victories, while controversy, scandal and drama have never been far away.

STORY

THE EARLY YEARS

In the early twentieth century, journalist and former bike racer Henri Desgrange was tasked with coming up with an idea to help boost sales of *L'Auto*, the sports newspaper created in 1899 as a breakaway from *Le Vélo* over disagreements about the Dreyfus Affair controversy that was dividing France at the time. With help from the paper's cycling reporter Géo Lefèvre, Desgrange devised a bike race on a scale that had never been seen before, in which those brave enough to enter would complete an entire tour around the nation of France. With that, the Tour de France was born.

These early editions following the race's inception in 1903 were considerably different from the race we know today, however, and over the years changes were gradually made. The rules were harsh back then, with restrictions on gearing and receiving help mending damaged equipment, and only in the 1920s were riders allowed to change a broken bike. A mixture of professionals and amateurs would take part, some as part of a sponsored team, others on their lonesome, all after the generous prize money on offer. In vying for victory, all sorts of cheating and shenanigans took place, from riders taking a tow from a car via a cork attached to a piece of string, to surreptitiously catching a train for part of the route, to fans on the roadside beating up the rivals of their favoured champion.

The race gained fame in this time as a brutal test of endeavour and endurance, and Desgrange and his team of organisers devised ever more sadistic ways to test the riders, most significantly by adding mountains to the route, first in the Vosges and the Alps, then, in 1910, to the Pyrenees. Interest spread across Europe, and riders from nations beyond France like Luxembourg, Belgium and Italy were successful. In 1920, Belgian Philippe Thys became the first rider to win three overall titles (and would probably have won more had the First World War not prevented the race from being run for four years), but in this era the race was better known for its spectacle than the individuals who won it.

By the time Desgrange passed away in 1940, the Tour had already long fulfilled its initial remit of increasing *L'Auto* sales (while *Le Vélo* had gone out of business), and had grown to become the biggest bike race in the world, and a national institution.

PREVIOUS PAGE

Crowds flock to the roadside of a mountain during an early edition of the Tour de France

MAIN IMAGE

Henri Desgrange

BELOW LEFT

Sylvere Maes repairs his bike after a puncture on Col du Galibier during stage 16 of the 1939 Tour de France, watched by Henri Desgrange

BELOW

Philippe Thys surrounded by spectators at the 1913 Tour de France

Philippe Thys

Philippe Thys was the first rider to win the Tour three times, a record that lasted for several decades before Louison Bobet eventually matched it in the 1950s. Unlike Bobet, Thys had to overcome all the extra challenges this early era of the Tour posed, from having to get his broken bike fixed at a local shop during the race, to incurring huge time penalties for unauthorised wheel changes. His career was interrupted between his second win in 1914 and his third in 1920 because of the First World War, and Henri Desgrange once remarked that he believed Thys could have won upwards of five Tours had it not been.

THE POST-WAR YEARS

When the Tour de France returned after a seven-year break for World War Two (now run by Desgrange's successor Jacques Goddet, for *L'Équipe*, the sports newspaper that took over after *L'Auto* was closed by the Allies for its pro-German stance during the occupation), a new era of star champions who transcended the sport was born. Italian Fausto Coppi, who won the race in 1949 and 1952, epitomised this; his stunning ability on the bike, coupled with a charismatic, scandalous personality, made him an international celebrity, while his rivalry with fellow Italian Gino Bartali became the stuff of legend. In 1953, France retook control of their race from the Italians and the Swiss (for whom Ferdinand Kübler and Hugo Koblet had won in 1950 and 1951 respectively) through Louison Bobet, a sensitive introvert who equalled Thys' record of three overall titles, and became the first to do so in successive years.

Bobet's achievements would be eclipsed in the 1960s, however, by Jacques Anquetil, the first ever winner of five Tours de France. This run of victories coincided with a change in 1962 regarding how teams were organised, from being nation-based to sponsor-based, and so Anquetil was in direct opposition to his French compatriot and great rival Raymond Poulidor. Anquetil always had the beating of him, as he did over other riders like Charly Gaul and Federico Bahamontes (winners in 1958 and 1959 respectively), who, though majestic climbers, lacked his all-round ability and ruthless mentality. He had a consistency and reliability that set him apart, was more capable on flat stages, and, above all, could gain enough time in the time trials to overturn whatever he might lose in the mountains. He was the first serial winner of the yellow jersey, and set the template that future champions would follow.

MAIN IMAGE

Fausto Coppi ascends the Col du Galibier during stage 11 of the 1952 Tour de France

BELOW RIGHT

Jacques Anquetil and Raymond Poulidor racing against each other, circa 1960

GREAT RIVALRIES

Much of the sporting drama of this era came from intense rivalries between opposing riders, which aroused great passion and polarisation among fans, and captured cultural differences and tensions that were present during this time of great social change in Europe. Among Italians, Gino Bartali and Fausto Coppi came to represent divisions in society after the defeat of Mussolini's fascist government, the devout Bartali the conservative rural south, Coppi the modernism of the north, especially after he courted scandal by having an extramarital affair.

In France, the public were similarly divided in the 1960s between Jacques Anquetil and Raymond Poulidor. Unlike Coppi and Bartali, who won two Tour titles each, this was a much more one-sided rivalry, with Anquetil winning five Tours, and Poulidor, nicknamed 'The Eternal Second', never even wearing the jersey in his career, let alone winning it. But it was this very underdog/champion dichotomy that made the rivalry what it was – while some admired Anquetil's ruthless efficiency, others found him too cold and cynical, and warmed more to 'Pou-Pou''s naive simplicity.

THE MERCKX ERA

In the years immediately after Jacques Anquetil's final finish in 1964, a power vacuum opened up at the Tour de France. The next four editions were each won by different first-time winners (Felice Gimondi, Lucien Aimar, Roger Pingeon and Jan Janssen), none of whom were able to go on and become multiple-champions.

That all changed in 1969, when a young Belgian named Eddy Merckx made his stupefyingly dominant debut at the Tour with a ride that would change cycling forever. Not content with simply winning the yellow jersey, he set out to win everything, and by a massive margin, embarking on a huge attack in the Pyrenees where the logical move would have been to ride defensively. It was a mindset that earned him the nickname of 'The Cannibal', and his ultimate winning margin of over 17 minutes was the biggest since Coppi's in 1952 and hasn't been bettered since, while he also became the only rider in history to win the yellow, green and polka-dot jerseys at the same race.

He once again won by a country mile defending his title in 1970, but came up against a worthy adversary the following year in Spaniard Luis Ocaña. Ocaña even managed to briefly take yellow from him with an attack in the mountains, before crashing out on a rainy descent in the Pyrenees, providing Merckx a clear run for his third title. A much-anticipated rematch was interrupted when Ocaña once again crashed out in 1972, but he did go on to win the yellow at next year's edition – albeit in the absence of Merckx.

After one more win in 1974 that equalled Anquetil's record of five, Merckx's run of uninterrupted dominance ended dramatically when a spectator punched him on the Puy-de-Dôme, inflicting injuries that would ultimately see him concede yellow to Bernard Thévenet. The subsequent years provided a chance for those who had suffered under the Belgian to achieve their own success, with four-time podium finisher Lucien Van Impe triumphing in 1976, and six-time runner-up Joop Zoetemelk at last claiming victory in 1980, while Thévenet won it again in 1977 – but still not poor Raymond Poulidor, who collected another three podium finishes in the 1970s to go with his five from the 1960s. Others flourished with Merckx out of the picture, with his Belgian rival Freddy Maertens winning a whopping eight stages and the points classification in 1976, but none would ever quite match his greatness.

FREDDY MAERTENS'S PROLIFIC 1976 TOUR

In 1976, Freddy Maertens bagged an enormous haul of eight stages, something that has only ever been done three other times in Tour history (the others being Charles Pelissier in 1930, and Eddy Merckx in 1970 and 1974). Even more remarkably, that was his Tour de France debut. The Belgian triumphed in three of the race's four individual time trials, then used his lethal finishing sprint to land another five road stages. Despite winning another couple in 1978, he only appeared in one more Tour afterwards as a dramatic loss of form mixed with personal problems of debt and alcoholism saw his career go off the rails, though he did mount an amazing comeback in 1981 to win another five stages.

LEFT

Eddy Merckx at the 1969 Tour de France

BELOW

Luis Ocaña and Eddy Merckx in the peloton during the 1975 Tour de France

THE HINAULT ERA

When Eddy Merckx retired from the sport in 1978, it seemed unlikely cycling would ever see his like again. But that very same year a new champion arrived at the Tour and announced himself as the great man's successor. Bernard Hinault had never ridden the Tour before, but that didn't stop him from running away with overall victory by almost four minutes. The next year was even more one-sided, with only Joop Zoetemelk finishing within 25 minutes of him, and although a knee injury forced him to abandon while leading the 1980 edition (allowing Zoetemelk to win instead), he went on to win again in 1981 and 1982 with little bother.

It wasn't just his talent that made Hinault such a colossal part of Tour history, but also his personality. Nicknamed 'The Badger' for his aggression, both on and off the bike, he was the 'patron' of the peloton, a figurehead who exerted influence in the sport whether through fear or respect. In terms of racing, though, his presence waned when he missed the 1983 Tour through injury, and placed second the next year behind the man who had triumphed in his absence, Laurent Fignon. A Parisian intellectual known for his bespectacled, urbane appearance, it seemed as though the young Fignon would supersede Hinault and dominate the Tour for years to come, but 'Le Professeur' suffered from injuries and a loss of form.

Instead, Hinault's main threat came from within his own team. American Greg LeMond may well have been strong enough to win the Tour ahead of his La Vie Claire teammate in 1985, but was under instruction to work for Hinault, meaning the Frenchman joined Anquetil and Merckx in the five-time winner club. To repay his loyalty, Hinault had promised to work for LeMond at the 1986 edition, but the way Hinault continued to attack throughout that race suggested he was after win number six. A truce was eventually called though, and LeMond became the first ever non-European to win the yellow jersey.

A freak hunting accident interrupted LeMond's career, and with Hinault having retired and Fignon still struggling for form, new winners emerged in Stephen Roche (1987) and Pedro Delgado (1988). But against the odds the American returned in 1989 to win the closest and possibly best Tour of all-time, ahead of a resurgent Fignon in an epic duel that went down to the final metres of the race. Another overall victory in 1990 followed for LeMond, before a new generation took over.

AN IRISH GOLDEN AGE

The 1980s were a golden era for Irish cycling; not only did Stephen Roche become the nation's first, and only, winner of the yellow jersey in a close battle in 1987, Sean Kelly was also one of the great riders of this generation. 'King Kelly' never quite had the climbing legs to win the yellow jersey, and was limited to a career-high overall finish of fourth, but he could do just about everything else, and has gone down as one of the sport's all-time great all-rounders, winning a total of four green jersey titles. His soothing voice and dry wit can now be heard on Eurosport, for whom he commentates at every Tour de France.

ABOVE
Greg LeMond in the yellow jersey and Bernard Hinault in the polka-dot jersey shake hands on the podium at the end of the 1986 Tour de France

RIGHT
Laurent Fignon and Greg LeMond climb the Côte de Laffrey during stage 18 of the 1989 Tour de France

THE INDURÁIN ERA

Miguel Induráin might not have had the larger-than-life personality of the previous five-time Tour de France winners, nor the same crowd-pleasingly entertaining racing style, but he was just as effective a winner. Between 1991 and 1995 he became the first rider to ever win five Tours in succession, and in none of those races did he ever really look like losing, never winning by less than three and a half minutes. Past winners, notably Bernard Hinault and Jacques Anquetil, had included time trials as a key part of their armoury, but none before had been quite so dependent as 'Big Mig.' His relatively heavy frame meant he was not a natural climber, and so he would make all his major gains in the time trial stages, and ride defensively in the mountains. It was a winning strategy that nobody could find a solution to, and although the likes of Claudio Chiappucci (second in 1992) and Tony Rominger (second in 1993) tried their best, Induráin never had a great rival to push him the way his forebears did.

When his reign as Tour champion did eventually end in 1996, it did so suddenly, as Induráin was shockingly dropped the very first summit finish of the race, losing a huge amount of ground and falling out of overall contention. Induráin was never the same again, and with him out of the picture, Dane Bjarne Riis went on to claim overall victory. Riis' young Team Telekom teammate Jan Ullrich inherited the title in 1997 at the age of just 23, while the beloved, but complicated, Marco Pantani triumphed in 1998 with the kind of attacking ride loved by the purists. However, all three of these victories have since been tarnished by doping revelations, and the messy, sometimes tragic direction their lives subsequently took (Pantani died of a cocaine overdose in 2004) reflects a sad chapter in cycling history.

ABOVE

Marco Pantani, wearing the yellow jersey and his trademark bandana, during stage 18 of the 1998 Tour de France

RIGHT

Miguel Induráin wears the yellow jersey during stage nine of the 1995 Tour de France

THE SPRINT TRAIN

The 1990s saw the birth of something that has since become a mainstay of the Tour de France, and road cycling in general: the sprint train. The Saeco team pioneered the technique, in which their teammates would lead the peloton in the final few kilometres of a sprint stage, and set such a fast pace that nobody could make a late attack out of the peloton, and that their sprinter Mario Cipollini would be in the perfect position to win the bunch sprint. In a straight up sprint like this, the charismatic playboy Cipollini was the quickest in the world, and won twelve stages throughout his career, more than anyone else in the decade. But, in what was also an era in which cyclists specialised in specific disciplines in a narrower way than they ever had before, the pure sprinter Cipollini couldn't handle the mountains, and never even finished the Tour, leaving slower sprinters but better all-rounders like Djamolidine Abdoujaparov and Erik Zabel to win the green jersey.

Banesto
Banesto

THE ARMSTRONG ERA

Ironically, when Lance Armstrong won his first Tour de France title in 1999, he was hailed as cycling's saviour in the aftermath of a doping scandal. The 1998 Tour had been scandalised by the Festina Affair, in which police investigations and raids uncovered doping products used by teams at the race. With an extraordinary comeback story from recovering from testicular cancer a few years earlier, and the potential, as an American, to be a global star spanning both sides of the Atlantic, Armstrong was welcomed as a new hero of the sport. Indeed, this was the birth of the Tour's latest star, as Armstrong won an unprecedented seven Tour titles, consecutively from 1999 to 2005. With help from his formidable US Postal Service teammates, he tormented his more vulnerable rivals Marco Pantani and Jan Ullrich with his steely mentality and indomitable will to win, and neither they nor later contenders Joseba Beloki or Ivan Basso could lay a glove on him.

Now, all seven of those victories have been struck from the record after an investigation from the United States Anti-Doping Agency concluded in 2012 that systematic doping had taken place in the US Postal Service team. Armstrong himself admitted his guilt, defending himself on the grounds that doping was widespread during this time; while that's true, nobody enforced the 'omerta' quite like him, who lied brazenly for years, and used his status to hound and silence whistle-blowers like Filippo Simeone, an Italian who testified against Armstrong's doctor and organiser of his doping program, Michele Ferrari.

The years after Armstrong's retirement were chaotic and characterised by controversy, as his former teammate (and later whistle-blower) Floyd Landis won the 2006 edition only to test positive (runner-up Óscar Pereiro is now credited as the official winner), and Michael Rasmussen was one of several riders kicked out during the 2007 edition while in the lead. The attack-minded climber Alberto Contador went on to win that year instead, and repeated that success in 2009 and 2010, only to also test positive during the latter. Andy Schleck was retrospectively handed the title, which thankfully remains the last time to date that a Tour winner has changed post facto.

A HISTORY OF DOPING

The Festina Affair and the Armstrong controversy are probably the most notorious doping scandals in cycling history, but it w as a problem that had blighted the sport for many decades before. Tom Simpson was the tragic victim of the doping culture of the 1960s, a time in which Jacques Anquetil once famously claimed that riders could not compete at the Tour de France on bread and water alone, while many of the most famous stars, including Eddy Merckx, failed tests for a variety of performance enhancing drugs in their careers. But doping was never as systematic as it was in the 1990 and 2000s, at which time the use of super-drugs like human growth hormones and EPO hugely increased speeds and grew out of control. It took the drug testers a while to catch up, but a significant decrease in scandals and positive tests over the last decade or so suggests the sport has cleaned up drastically.

ABOVE
Tom Simpson wearing the rainbow jersey as world champion, a title won in 1965, just two years before his tragic death climbing Mont Ventoux

ABOVE

Lance Armstrong puts on a raincoat while riding in front of German Jan Ullrich during the seventh stage of 2005 Tour de France

THE BRITISH ERA

Team Sky first appeared at the Tour de France at the start of the 2010s to much fanfare, but little impact. They had yet had the chance to invest the significant budget at their disposal, and were nowhere to be seen in the race for overall victory, as Cadel Evans instead became the first ever Australian to win the yellow jersey in 2011. But by 2012 they had assembled and organised a well-drilled line-up chock full of talent, and controlled the race from start to finish, with Bradley Wiggins ultimately placing first and Chris Froome second, making them the first team since Telekom in 1996 to occupy both top steps of the podium.

It was a watershed moment in British cycling (that had never before seen a rider make the podium before, let alone win), and turned out to be the beginning of a glorious eight-year run of success for the team, interrupted only once by Vincenzo Nibali in 2014, who capitalised after Froome crashed out. Froome was the talisman of their reign, taking over the leadership from Wiggins in 2013 with a resounding victory over Colombian climbing specialist Nairo Quintana, who he again got the better of in 2015 to win a second Tour title, despite a dangerous attack on Alpe d'Huez during the race's penultimate stage. The lightweight Quintana might have been able to give him problems in the mountains, but Froome had a vastly superior time trial, and was always extremely well protected by his black-clad Sky teammates, who prevented rivals from attacking with their metronomic pace-setting in the mountains. That, coupled with his ruthless streak and level-headed ability to remain calm under pressure, saw Froome comfortably win another two yellow jerseys in 2016 and 2017, bringing him to within one title of the joint record.

That fifth title would prove elusive for him personally, but not for Team Sky, as Welshman Geraint Thomas was victorious in 2018, with Froome placing third. Froome still hoped to reassert himself as the team's main man, but a horrible crash while preparing for the 2019 Tour de France scuppered his hopes. He's never been the same since, and parted ways with the team in 2020.

Colombian Egan Bernal emerged as his apparent successor when he won the Tour in 2019, but he's since been blighted by his own injury problems. Instead, the Tour entered a new era defined by the great rivalry between Tadej Pogačar and Jonas Vingegaard, who last year became the first pair of riders in history to occupy first and second on GC for four successive Tours. With many more exciting young riders emerging, such as Remco Evenepoel, there are many more chapters of the Tour de France still to be written.

Bradley Wiggins

As the year that London hosted the summer Olympics, 2012 was a golden year for British sport, and Bradley Wiggins was its poster boy. Prior to winning Olympic gold in the time trial, he captured the imagination of the nation by winning the yellow jersey. On paper, it appeared he had won comfortably, taking the yellow jersey towards the end of the first week, and defending it all the way to Paris to win by a margin of over three minutes. But behind the scenes Wiggins was struggling, and even thought about quitting during the second week after his teammate Froome appeared to purposefully drop him during the mountain top finish at La Toussuire. Unlike Froome, who was so at ease with himself during his reign as Tour champion, Wiggins struggled with the demands of competing for the yellow jersey and the fame that came with it. 2012 was to be his last ever appearance, but not before he'd already made British history, and won the nation's hearts.

MAIN IMAGE

Chris Froome leads Bradley Wiggins, in yellow, as they climb La Toussuire during stage 11 of the 2012 Tour de France

BELOW RIGHT

Bradley Wiggins, dressed in the yellow jersey, celebrates having won stage 19 of the 2012 Tour de France

MARK CAVENDISH: RECORD BREAKER

At stage five of last year's race, at the otherwise nondescript small town of Saint-Vulbas, Tour de France history was made. By sprinting to victory for the 35th time in his career, Mark Cavendish broke the record for the most career Tour de France stage wins, surpassing the great Eddy Merckx's record that had stood for almost fifty years. It was a record that many believed to be unsurpassable, but the special blend of stubborn determination, longevity, resilience to bounce back from countless setbacks, and sheer speed on the bike that had already made Cavendish the greatest sprinter of all time ultimately saw him capture the prize he spent years hunting.

The achievement was made all the more special for the fact that just a few days earlier Cavendish was on the brink of having to leave the race altogether. He fell badly ill on the very first day of the race as a consequence of the heat, and, vomiting and in some distress, barely managed to make it to the finish within the time limit. But he somehow summoned the strength to pull through, and made a full recovery once the heat died down to mount yet another miraculous comeback in a career defined by them.

It was clear from his celebrations in Saint-Vulbas just how much breaking the record meant not just for Cavendish, but for his colleagues too. The Manxman has always worn his emotions on his sleeve, and here he wore an irrepressible grin as he hugged his teammates and loved-ones, before a teary-eyed post-race interview. He is also notoriously spikey, and does not suffer fools gladly – woe betide the journalist who asks him a lazy question at a press conference. Yet the way his fellow riders responded to his win, each one going up to offer sincere congratulations, showed just how well-liked and respected he is in the peloton. He's a man who sets impeccably high standards for himself and everyone around him, and for those who meet those standards, he is strikingly open, passionate, intelligent and loyal.

These personality traits are part of what made Cavendish's career an unprecedented success. The so-called 'Manx Missile' is a force of nature, someone who combines staunch self-belief with resolute determination to get the best out of himself. He was outspoken and brash at his first Tour de France in 2008, at the age of just 23, but backed it up by winning four stages. At the same time, though, he was thoughtful and appreciative, quick to laud his teammates for their exemplary work leading him out in the final kilometres. He was even more prolific the next year, storming his way to a whopping six stage wins (which remains the most a sprinter has won at a Tour de France since the 1970s), and continued to be unstoppable in the bunch finishes the following year when he accumulated another five. Then in 2011, along with another five stages, he also won the green jersey for the first time in his career, having missed out by frustratingly narrow margins in the previous editions.

These were the peak years of Cavendish's career, but he continued to tot up the wins even as the competition improved. His former teammate André Greipel and the young Peter Sagan both equalled his tally of three in 2012, meaning that for the first time he was not the outright dominant sprinter at the Tour de France. German Marcel Kittel then burst onto the scene in

MAIN IMAGE
Mark Cavendish has cycled his way into the record books

Columb
TC

LIMAR
LUTSENKO
LIMAR
ASTANA QAZAQSTAN
Wilier
SAMRUK
KAZYNA
LUTSENKO
LUTSENKO
196
196

2013 and relegated him to a clear second best, but Cavendish still managed another two wins. A crash on the opening stage of the 2014 edition prevented him from reasserting himself as the top sprinter, but he returned in 2015 to win another stage, albeit in the shadow of an excelling Griepel, who amassed four wins for himself.

It was in 2016 that Cavendish mounted the first of his improbable comebacks. Now the wrong side of 30 and facing competition from the younger generation, it seemed his best years were behind him. But he ended up enjoying his best Tour de France for years, winning the opening stage in Normandy to wear the yellow jersey for the first time in his career, and going on to land three more wins.

In 2017, he was diagnosed with the Epstein-Barr virus, a debilitating, lingering condition of chronic fatigue that sapped away at his strength and looked as though it would bring a premature end to his glittering career. Where once he had been the quickest sprinter in the world, and possibly the best of all time, now he was barely able to compete at all in the bunch finishes, a shadow of his former self to whom age was also catching up.

By 2021, having gone over three whole years without a win of any kind, practically everybody had written him off ever winning at the Tour again. Cavendish himself, though, had not given up hope, and that year came his second great revival, even more extraordinary than the last. Having missed the last two Tours altogether, merely appearing at the race was a triumph, but he did so much more than just that. On the fourth stage, against all the odds, he stormed to a memorable victory in Fougères, an emotionally overwhelming moment for both himself and fans of the sport. And that wasn't all. He went on to dominate the sprints in that race, adding a second, third and fourth victory, and even the green jersey for only the second time in his career. It wasn't just an improbable return to form – in some ways, at the grand age of 36, he was even better than ever.

Those four wins saw him draw level with Merckx's record of 34 Tour wins and, though downplaying its importance to him to the media, it became his final career ambition. Yet again, he was thwarted by setbacks. His form dipped the following year, and his Quick-Step team did not select him in their Tour line-up. That prompted him to move to the Astana team, where he was guaranteed selection, but ended in tears when he crashed out of the race in the first week. That had meant to be his last race before retiring for good, but it was such a heartbreaking way for his career to end that he decided to give it one more shot the following year. And thank goodness he did, coming back the following year to take that elusive 35th win, and thus completing one of the all-time greatest careers, not just in cycling, but in any sport.

TOUR DE FRANCE WINNERS LISTED BY YEAR

YEAR	RIDER	TEAM	STAGE WINS	MARGIN
2024	Tadej Pogačar (Slo)	UAE Team Emirates	6	6-17
2023	Jonas Vingegaard (Den)	Jumbo-Visma	1	7-29
2022	Jonas Vingegaard (Den)	Jumbo-Visma	2	2-43
2021	Tadej Pogačar (Slo)	UAE Team Emirates	3	5-20
2020	Tadej Pogačar (Slo)	UAE Team Emirates	3	0-59
2019	Egan Bernal (Col)	Ineos	0	1-11
2018	Geraint Thomas (GBR)	Sky	2	1-51
2017	Chris Frome (GBR)	Sky	0	0-54
2016	Chris Frome (GBR)	Sky	2	4-05
2015	Chris Frome (GBR)	Sky	1	1-12
2014	Vincenzo Nibali (Ita)	Astana	4	7-37
2013	Chris Frome (GBR)	Sky	3	4-20
2012	Bradley Wiggins (GBR)	Sky	2	3-21
2011	Cadel Evans (Aus)	BMC	1	1-34
2010	Andy Schleck (Lux)	Saxo Bank	2	1-22
2009	Alberto Contador (Spa)	Astana	2	4-11
2008	Carlos Sastre (Spa)	CSC	1	0-58
2007	Alberto Contador (Spa)	Discovery Channel	1	0-23
2006	Óscar Pereiro (Spa)	*C.E.I.B.	0	0-32
2005	No winner			
2004	No winner			
2003	No winner			
2002	No winner			
2001	No winner			
2000	No winner			
1999	No winner			
1998	Marco Pantani (Ita)	Mercatone Uno-Bianchi	2	3-21
1997	Jan Ullrich (Ger)	Telekom	2	9-09
1996	Bjarne Riis (Den)	Telekom	2	1-41
1995	Miguel Induráin (Spa)	Banesto	2	4-35
1994	Miguel Induráin (Spa)	Banesto	1	5-39
1993	Miguel Induráin (Spa)	Banesto	2	4-59
1992	Miguel Induráin (Spa)	Banesto	3	4-35
1991	Miguel Induráin (Spa)	Banesto	2	3-36
1990	Greg LeMond (USA)	Z-Tomasso	0	2-16
1989	Greg LeMond (USA)	*AD.R.W.C.B.	3	0-08
1988	Pedro Delgado (Spa)	Reynolds	1	7-13
1987	Stephen Roche (Irl)	Carrera Jeans-Vagabond	1	0-40
1986	Greg LeMond (USA)	La Vie Claire	1	3-10
1985	Bernard Hinault (Fra)	La Vie Claire	2	1-42
1984	Laurent Fignon (Fra)	Renault-Elf	5	10-32
1983	Laurent Fignon (Fra)	Renault-Elf	1	4-04
1982	Bernard Hinault (Fra)	Renault-Elf-Gitane	4	6-21
1981	Bernard Hinault (Fra)	Renault-Elf-Gitane	5	14-34
1980	Joop Zoetemelk (Ned)	TI-Raleigh-Creda	2	6-55
1979	Bernard Hinault (Fra)	Renault-Gitane	7	13-07
1978	Bernard Hinault (Fra)	*R.G.C.	3	3-56
1977	Bernard Thévenet (Fra)	Peugeot-Esso-Michelin	1	0-48
1976	Lucien Van Impe (Bel)	Gitane-Campagnolo	1	4-14
1975	Bernard Thévenet (Fra)	Peugeot-BP-Michelin	2	2-47
1974	Eddy Merckx (Bel)	Molteni	8	8-04
1973	Luis Ocaña (Spa)	Bic	6	15-51
1972	Eddy Merckx (Bel)	Molteni	6	10-41
1971	Eddy Merckx (Bel)	Molteni	4	9-51
1970	Eddy Merckx (Bel)	Faemino-Faema	8	12-41
1969	Eddy Merckx (Bel)	Faema	6	17-54
1968	Jan Janssen (Ned)	Pelforth-Sauvage-Lejune	2	0-38
1967	Roger Pingeon (Fra)	France	1	3-40
1966	Lucian Aimar (Fra)	Ford-France-Hutchinson	0	1-07
1965	Felice Gimondi (Ita)	Salvarani	3	2-40
1964	Jacques Anquetil (Fra)	*S.R.G.C.	4	0-55
1963	Jacques Anquetil (Fra)	St Raphael-Gitane-Dunlop	4	3-35
1962	Jacques Anquetil (Fra)	*S.R.H.H	2	4-59
1961	Jacques Anquetil (Fra)	France	2	12-14
1960	Gastone Nencini (Ita)	Italy	0	5-02
1959	Federico Bahamontes (Spa)	Spain	1	4-01
1958	Charly Gaul (Lux)	Luxembourg	4	3-10
1957	Jacques Anquetil (Fra)	France	4	14-56
1956	Roger Walkowiak (Fra)	France	0	1-25
1955	Louison Bobet (Fra)	France	2	4-53
1954	Louison Bobet (Fra)	France	3	15-49
1953	Louison Bobet (Fra)	France	2	14-18
1952	Fausto Coppo (Ita)	Italy	5	28-17
1951	Hugo Koblet (Swi)	Switzerland	5	22-00
1950	Ferdinand Kübler (Swi)	Switzerland	3	9-30
1949	Fausto Coppi (Ita)	Italy	3	10-55
1948	Gino Bartali (Ita)	Italy	7	26-52
1947	Jean Robic (Fra)	France	3	3-58
1946	Not held			
1945	Not held			
1944	Not held			
1943	Not held			
1942	Not held			
1941	Not held			
1940	Not held			
1939	Sylvère Maes (Bel)	Belgium	2	30-38
1938	Gino Bartali (Ita)	Italy	2	18-27
1937	Roger Lapébie (Fra)	France	3	7-17
1936	Sylvère Maes (Bel)	Belgium	4	26-55
1935	Romain Maes (Bel)	Belgium	3	17-52
1934	Antonin Magne (Bel)	France	3	27-31
1933	Georges Speicher (Fra)	France	3	4-01
1932	André Leducq (Fra)	France	6	24-03
1931	Antonin Magne (Bel)	France	1	12-56
1930	André Leducq (Fra)	France	2	14-13
1929	Maurice De Waele (Bel)	Alcyon-Dunlop	1	44-23
1928	Nicolas Frantz (Lux)	Alcyon-Dunlop	5	50-07
1927	Nicolas Frantz (Lux)	Alcyon-Dunlop	3	1-48-21
1926	Lucien Buysse (Bel)	Automoto-Hutchinson	2	1-22-25
1925	Ottavio Bottecchia (Ita)	Automato-Hutchinson	4	54-20
1924	Ottavio Bottecchia (Ita)	Automato	4	35-36
1923	Henri Pélissier (Fra)	Automato	3	30-41
1922	Firmin Lambot (Bel)	Peugeot-Wolber	0	41-15
1921	Léon Scieur (Bel)	La Sportive	2	18-36
1920	Philippe Thys (Bel)	La Sportive	4	57-21
1919	Firmin Lambot (Bel)	La Sportive	1	1-42-54
1918	Not held			
1917	Not held			
1916	Not held			
1915	Not held			
1914	Philippe Thys (Bel)	Peugeot-Wolber	1	1-50
1913	Philippe Thys (Bel)	Peugeot-Wolber	1	8-37
1912	Odile Defraye (Bel)	Alcyon	3	-
1911	Gustave Garrigou (Fra)	Alcyon	2	-
1910	Octave Lapize (Fra)	Alcyon	4	-
1909	François Faber (Lux)	Alcyon	6	-
1908	Lucien Petit-Breton (Fra)	Peugeot-Wolber	5	-
1907	Lucien Petit-Breton (Fra)	Peugeot-Wolber	2	-
1906	René Pottier (Fra)	Peugeot-Wolber	5	-
1905	Louis Trousselier (Fra)	Peugeot-Wolber	5	-
1904	Henri Cornet (Fra)	Conte	1	2-16-14
1903	Maurice Garin (Fra)	La Française	3	2-59-21

TOUR DE FRANCE POINTS CLASSIFICATION WINNERS LISTED BY YEAR

YEAR	RIDER	TEAM	POINTS
2024	Biniam Girmay (Eri)	Intermarché-Wanty	387
2023	Jasper Philipsen (Bel)	Alpecin-Deceuninck	377
2022	Wout van Aert (Bel)	Jumbo-Visma	480

YEAR	RIDER	TEAM	POINTS
2021	Mark Cavendish (GBR)	Deceuninck-QuickStep	337
2020	Sam Bennett (Irl)	Deceuninck-QuickStep	380
2019	Peter Sagan (Svk)	Bora-Hansgrohe	316
2018	Peter Sagan (Svk)	Bora-Hansgrohe	477
2017	Michael Matthews (Aus)	Sunweb	370
2016	Peter Sagan (Svk)	Tinkoff	470
2015	Peter Sagan (Svk)	Tinkoff-Saxo	432
2014	Peter Sagan (Svk)	Cannondale	431
2013	Peter Sagan (Svk)	Cannondale	409
2012	Peter Sagan (Svk)	Liquigas-Cannondale	421
2011	Mark Cavendish (GBR)	HTC-Highroad	334
2010	Alessandro Petacchi (Ita)	Lampre-Farnese	243
2009	Thor Hushovd (Nor)	Cervelo	280
2008	Óscar Freire (Spa)	Rabobank	270
2007	Tom Boonen (Bel)	Quick Step-Innergetic	256
2006	Robbie McEwen (Aus)	Davitamon-Lotto	272
2005	Thor Hushovd (Nor)	Credit Agricole	194
2004	Robbie McEwen (Aus)	Lotto-Domo	272
2003	Baden Cooke (Aus)	fdjeux.com	216
2002	Robbie McEwan (Aus)	Lotto-Adecco	280
2001	Erik Zabel (Ger)	Telekom	252
2000	Erik Zabel (Ger)	Telekom	321
1999	Erik Zabel (Ger)	Telekom	323
1998	Erik Zabel (Ger)	Telekom	327
1997	Erik Zabel (Ger)	Telekom	350
1996	Erik Zabel (Ger)	Telekom	335
1995	Laurent Jalabert (Fra)	ONCE	333
1994	Djamolidine Abdoujaparov (Uzb)	Polti	322
1993	Djamolidine Abdoujaparov (Uzb)	Lampre-Polti	298
1992	Laurent Jalabert (Fra)	ONCE	293
1991	Djamolidine Abdoujaparov (URS)	Carrera Jeans	316
1990	Olaf Ludwig (Ger)	Panasonic-Sportlife	256
1989	Sean Kelly (Irl)	PDM	277
1988	Eddy Planckaert (Bel)	A.D.R – I.O.C	278
1987	Jean-Paul van Poppel (Ned)	*S.K.Y.C.	263
1986	Eric Vanderaraerden (Bel)	Panasonic	277
1985	Sean Kelly (Irl)	Skil-Sem-Kas-Miko	434
1984	Frank Hoste (Bel)	*B.D.E.D.E.M.	322
1983	Sean Kelly (Irl)	Sem-Mavic-Reydel	360
1982	Sean Kelly (Irl)	*S.F.L.C.	429
1981	Freddy Maertens (Bel)	Sunair-Colnago	428
1980	Rudy Pevenage (Bel)	*I.W.K.M.	194
1979	Bernard Hinault (Fra)	Renault Gitane	263
1978	Freddy Maertens (Bel)	Velda-Lano-Flandria	242
1977	Jacques Esclassan (Fra)	Peugeot-Esso-Michelin	236
1976	Freddy Maertens (Bel)	Flandria-Velda-Vleesbedrijf	293
1975	Rik Van Linden (Bel)	Bianchi	342
1974	Patrick Sercu (Bel)	Brooklyn	283
1973	Herman Van Springel (Bel)	Rokado	187
1972	Eddy Merckx (Bel)	Molteni	196
1971	Eddy Merckx (Bel)	Molteni	202
1970	Walter Godefroot (Bel)	Faema-Faemino	212
1969	Eddy Merckx (Bel)	Faema	244
1968	Franco Bitossi (Ita)	Italy	241
1967	Jan Janssen (Ned)	Netherlands	154
1966	Willy Planckaert (Bel)	Ford-France-Hutchinson	211
1965	Jan Janssen (Ned)	*P.S.L.W.	144
1964	Jan Janssen (Ned)	*P.S.L.W.	208
1963	Rik Van Looy (Bel)	G.B.C-Libertas	275
1962	Rudi Altig (Ger)	*S.R.H.H.	173
1961	André Darrigade (Fra)	France	174
1960	Jean Graczyk (Fra)	France	74
1959	André Darrigade (Fra)	France	613
1958	Jean Graczyk (Fra)	Centre-Midi	347
1957	Jean Forestier (Fra)	France	301
1956	Stan Ockers (Bel)	Belgium	280
1955	Stan Ockers (Bel)	Belgium	322
1954	Ferdinand Kübler (Swi)	Switzerland	215.5
1953	Fritz Schär (Swi)	Switzerland	271

TOUR DE FRANCE KING OF THE MOUNTAINS WINNERS LISTED BY YEAR

YEAR	RIDER	TEAM	POINTS
2024	Richard Carapaz (Ecu)	EF Education-EasyPost	127
2023	Giulio Ciccone (Ita)	Trek-Segafredo	106
2022	Jonas Vingegaard (Den)	Jumbo-Visma	72
2021	Tadej Pogačar (Slo)	UAE Team Emirates	107
2020	Tadej Pogačar (Slo)	UAE Team Emirates	82
2019	Romain Barder (Fra)	Ag2r La Mondiale	86
2018	Julian Alaphilippe (Fra)	QuickStep-Floors	170
2017	Warren Barguil (Fra)	Sunweb	169
2016	Rafał Majka (Pol)	Tinkoff	209
2015	Chris Froome (GBR)	Sky	119
2014	Rafał Majka (Pol)	Tinkoff-Saxo	181
2013	Nairo Quintana (Col)	Movistar	147
2012	Thomas Voeckler (Fra)	Europcar	135
2011	Samuel Sanchez (Spa)	Euskaltel-Euskadi	108
2010	Anthony Charteau (Fra)	BBox Bouygues Telecom	143
2009	Franco Pellizotti (Ita)	Liquigas	210
2008	Carlos Sastre (Spa)	CSC Saxo Bank	80
2007	Juan Mauricio Soler (Col)	Barloworld	206
2006	Michael Rasmussen (Den)	Rabobank	166
2005	Michael Rasmussen (Den)	Rabobank	185
2004	Richard Virenque (Fra)	QuickStep-Davitamon	226
2003	Richard Virenque (Fra)	QuickStep-Davitamon	324
2002	Laurent Jalabert (Fra)	CSC-Tiscali	262
2001	Laurent Jalabert (Fra)	CSC-Tiscali	258
2000	Santiago Botero (Col)	Kelme-Costa Blanca	347
1999	Richard Virenque (Fra)	Polti	279
1998	Christophe Rlbero (Fra)	Cofidis	200
1997	Richard Virenque (Fra)	Festina	579
1996	Richard Virenque (Fra)	Festina	383
1995	Richard Virenque (Fra)	Festina	438
1994	Richard Virenque (Fra)	Festina-Andorra	392
1993	Tony Rominger (Swi)	Clas-Cajastur	449
1992	Claudio Chiappucci (Ita)	Carrera Jeans-Tassoni	410
1991	Claudio Chiappucci (Ita)	Carrera Jeans-Tassoni	312
1990	Thierry Claveyrolat (Fra)	RMO-Mavic-Liberia	321
1989	Gert-Jan Theunisse (Ned)	PDM	441
1988	Steven Rooks (Ned)	PDM	326
1987	Lucho Herrera (Col)	Café de Colombia	452
1986	Bernard Hinault (Fra)	La Vie Claire	351
1985	Lucho Herrera (Col)	Café de Colombia	440

*C.E.I.B. = Caisse d'Epargne-Illes Balears
*AD.R.W.C.B. = AD Renting-W-Cup-Bottecchia
*R.G.C. = Renault-Girane-Campagnolo
*S.R.H.H. = St Raphael-Helyett-Hutchinson
*S.R.G.C. = St Raphael-Gitane-Campagnolo
*S.K.Y.C. = Superconfex-Kwantum-Yoko-Colnago
*B.D.E.D.E.M. = Boule D'or-Europ Decor-Eddy Merckx
*S.F.L.C. = Sem-France Loire-Campagnolo
*I.W.K.M. = Ijsboerke-Warncke-Koga Miyata
*P.S.L.W. = Pelforth-Sauvage-Lejeune-Wolber

YEAR	RIDER	TEAM	POINTS
1984	Philippa York (GBR)	Peugeot-Shell-Michelin	284
1983	Lucien Van Impe (Bel)	Metaurobili-Pinarello	272
1982	Bernard Vallet (Fra)	La Redoute-Motobecane	278
1981	Lucien Van Impe (Bel)	Boston-Mavic	284
1980	Raymond Martin (Fra)	Miko-Mercier-Vivagel	223
1979	Giovanni Battaglin (Ita)	Inoxpran	239
1978	Mariano Martinez (Fra)	Jobo-Superia	187
1977	Lucien Van Impe (Bel)	Lejeune-BP	244
1976	Giancarlo Bellini (Ita)	Brooklyn-Gios	170
1975	Lucien Van Impe (Bel)	Gitane	285
1974	Domingo Perurena (Spa)	Kas-Kaskol	171
1973	Pedro Torres (Spa)	La Casera-Bahamontes	225
1972	Lucien Van Impe (Bel)	Sonolor	229
1971	Lucien Van Impe (Bel)	Sonolor	228
1970	Eddy Merckx (Bel)	Faema-Faemino	128
1969	Eddy Merckx (Bel)	Faema	155
1968	Aurelio Gonzalez (Spa)	Spain	98
1967	Julio Jimenez (Spa)	Spain	122
1966	Julio Jimenez (Spa)	Ford-France-Hutchinson	123
1965	Julio Jimenez (Spa)	Kas-Kaskol	133
1964	Federico Bahamontes (Spa)	Margnat-Paloma-Dunlop	173
1963	Federico Bahamontes (Spa)	*M.P.M.D.	147
1962	Federico Bahamontes (Spa)	*M.P.D.A.	137
1961	Imerio Massignan (Ita)	Italy	95
1960	Imerio Massignan (Ita)	Italy	56
1959	Federico Bahamontes (Spa)	Spain	73
1958	Federico Bahamontes (Spa)	Spain	79
1957	Gastone Nencini (Ita)	Italy	44
1956	Charly Gaul (Lux)	Luxembourg-Mixed	71
1955	Charly Gaul (Lux)	Luxembourg-Mixed	84
1954	Federico Bahamontes (Spa)	Spain	95
1953	Jesús Loroño (Spa)	Spain	54
1952	Fausto Coppi (Ita)	Italy	92
1951	Raphaël Géminiani (Fra)	France	66
1950	Louison Bobet (Fra)	France	58
1949	Fausto Coppi (Ita)	Italy	81
1948	Gino Bartali (Ita)	Italy	62
1947	Pierre Brambilla (Ita)	Italy	98
1946	Not held		
1945	Not held		
1944	Not held		
1943	Not held		
1942	Not held		
1941	Not held		
1940	Not held		
1939	Sylvère Maes (Bel)	Belgium	85
1938	Gino Bartali (Ita)	Italy	107
1937	Félicien Vervaecke (Bel)	Belgium	114
1936	Julian Berrendero (Spain-Luxembourg		1936
1935	Félicien Vervaecke (Bel)	Belgium	118
1934	René Vietto (Fra)	France	111
1933	Vicente Trueba (Spa)	Touristes-Routiers	134

TOUR DE FRANCE YOUNG RIDER CLASSIFICATION WINNERS LISTED BY YEAR

YEAR	RIDER	TEAM	MARGIN
2024	Remco Evenepoel (Bel)	Soudal-QuickStep	15-46
2023	Tadej Pogačar (Slo)	UAE Team Emirates	5-48
2022	Tadej Pogačar (Slo)	UAE Team Emirates	58-32
2021	Tadej Pogačar (Slo)	UAE Team Emirates	5-20
2020	Tadej Pogačar (Slo)	UAE Team Emirates	6-07
2019	Egan Bernal (Col)	Ineos	23-58
2018	Pierre Latour (Fra)	Ag2r La Mondiale	5-39
2017	Simon Yates (GBR)	Orica-Scott	2-06
2016	Adam Yates (GBR)	Orica-BikeExchange	2-16
2015	Nairo Quintana (Col)	Movistar	14-48
2014	Thibaut Pinot (Fra)	FDJ.FR	3-11
2013	Nairo Quintana (Col)	Movistar	13-19
2012	Tejay van Garderen (USA)	BMC	6-13
2011	Pierre Rolland (Fra)	Europcar	0-46
2010	Andy Schleck (Lux)	Saxo Bank	8-52
2009	Andy Schleck (Lux)	Saxo Bank	3-24
2008	Andy Schleck (Lux)	CSC Saxo-Bank	1-27
2007	Alberto Contador (Spa)	Discovery Channel	16-51
2006	Damiano Cunego (Ita)	Lampre-Fondital	0-38
2005	Yaroslav Popovych (Ukr)	Discovery Channel	9-02
2004	Vladimir Karpets (Rus)	Illes Balears-B. Santander	3-42
2003	Denis Menchov (Rus)	iBanesto.com	42-29
2002	Ivan Basso (Ita)	Fassa Bortolo	13-26
2001	Óscar Sevilla (Spa)	Kelme-Costa Blanca	10-03
2000	Francisco Mancebo (Spa)	Banesto	17-48
1999	Benoît Salmon (Fra)	Casino	10-22
1998	Jan Ullrich (Ger)	Telekom	5-55
1997	Jan Ullrich (Ger)	Telekom	45-39
1996	Jan Ullrich (Ger)	Telekom	5-26
1995	Marco Pantani (Ita)	Carrera Jeans-Tassoni	8-29
1994	Marco Pantani (Ita)	Carrera Jeans-Tassoni	2-51
1993	Antonio Martin (Spa)	Amaya Seguros	3-28
1992	Eddy Bouwmans (Ned)	Panasonic-Sportlife	17-26
1991	Álvaro Mejía (Col)	Postobón	20-55
1990	Gilles Delion (Fra)	Helvetia-La Suisse	13-41
1989	Fabrice Philipot (Fra)	Toshiba	0-59
1988	Erik Breukink (Ned)	Panasonic-Isostar	8-08
1987	Raúl Alcalá (Mex)	7-Eleven	31-46
1986	Andrew Hampsten (USA)	La Vie Claire	7-15
1985	Fabio Parra (Col)	Café de Colombia-Mavic	0-21
1984	Greg LeMond (USA)	Renault-Elf	14-31
1983	Laurent Fignon (Fra)	Renault-Elf	4-04
1982	Phil Anderson (Aus)	Peugeot-Shell-Michelin	19-41
1981	Peter Winnen (Ned)	Capri Sonne-Koga Miyata	5-52
1980	Johan van der Velde (Ned)	TI-Raleigh-Creda	2-15
1979	Jean-René Bernaudeau (Fra)	Renault-Gitane	7-55
1978	Henk Lubberding (Ned)	TI-Raleigh-McGregor	5-34
1977	Dietrich Thurau (Ger)	TI-Raleigh	15-07
1976	Enrique Martínez Heredia (Spa)	Kas-Campagnolo	1-30
1975	Francesco Moser (Ita)	Filotex	16-32

TOUR DE FRANCE WINNERS' STATISTICS

OVERALL RIDER VICTORIES	STAGE	WINS	SEASONS
1. Jacques Anquetil (Fra)	5	16	1957, 1961, 1962, 1963, 1964
2. Eddy Merckx (Bel)	5	34	1969, 1970, 1971, 1972, 1974
3. Bernard Hinault (Fra)	5	28	1978, 1979, 1981, 1982, 1985
4. Miguel Induráin (Spa)	5	12	1991, 1992, 1993, 1994, 1995
5. Chris Froome (GBR)	4	7	2013, 2015, 2016, 2017
6. Philippe Thys (Bel)	3	13	1913, 1914, 1920
7. Loison Bobet (Fra)	3	11	1953, 1954, 1955

* *M.P.M.D. = Margnat-Paloma-Motul-Dunlop
*M.P.D.A. = Margnat-Paloma-D'Alessandro

	RIDER	OVERALL VICTORIES	STAGE WINS	SEASONS
8.	Greg LeMond (USA)	3	5	1986, 1989, 1990
9.	Tadej Pogačar (Slo)	3	17	2020, 2021, 2024
10.	Lucien Petit-Breton (Fra)	2	7	1907, 1908
11.	Firmin Lambot (Bel)	2	6	1919, 1922
12.	Ottavio Bottecchia (Ita)	2	9	1924, 1925
13.	Nicolas Frantz (Lux)	2	20	1927, 1928
14.	André Leducq (Fra)	2	25	1930, 1932
15.	Antonin Magne (Fra)	2	10	1931, 1934
16.	Sylvère Maes (Bel)	2	9	1936, 1939
17.	Gino Bartali (Ita)	2	12	1938, 1948
18.	Fausto Coppi (Ita)	2	9	1949, 1952
19.	Bernard Thévenet (Fra)	2	9	1975, 1977
20.	Laurent Fignon (Fra)	2	9	1983, 1984
21.	Alberto Contador (Spa)	2	3	2007, 2009
22.	Jonas Vingegaard (Den)	2	3	2022, 2023

RIDERS WITH THE MOST TOUR DE FRANCE WINS

	RIDER	TOTAL CAREER STAGE WINS
1.	Mark Cavendish (GBR)	35
2.	Eddy Merckx (Bel)	34
3.	Bernard Hinault (Fra)	28
4.	André Leducq (Fra)	25
5.	André Darrigade (Fra)	22
6.	Nicolas Frantz (Lux)	20
7.	François Faber (Lux)	19
8.	Jean Alavoine (Fra)	17
9.	Tadej Pogačar (Slo)	17
10.	Jacques Anquetil (Fra)	16
11.	René Le Grevès (Fra)	16
12.	Charles Pélissier (Fra)	16
13.	Freddy Maertens (Bel)	15
14.	Marcel Kittel (Ger)	14
15.	Philippe Thys (Bel)	13
16.	Louis Trousselier (Fra)	13
17.	Gino Bartali (Ita)	12
18.	Mario Cipollini (Ita)	12
19.	Miguel Indurain (Spa)	12
20.	Robbie McEwen (Aus)	12
21.	Peter Sagan (Svk)	12
22.	Erik Zabel (Ger)	12
23.	Jean Aerts (Bel)	11
24.	Louison Bobet (Fra)	11
25.	Raffaele Di Paco (Ita)	11
26.	André Greipel (Ger)	11
27.	Maurice Archambaud (Fra)	10
28.	Charly Gaul (Lux)	10
29.	Walter Godefroot (Bel)	10
30.	Thor Hushovd (Nor)	10
31.	Gerrie Knetemann (Ned)	10
32.	Antonin Magne (Fra)	10
33.	Henri Pélissier (Fra)	10
34.	Jan Raas (Ned)	10
35.	Joop Zoetemelk (Ned)	10

Picture credits

The publishers would like to thank the following sources for their kind permission to reproduce the pictures in this book.

pp4-5 Joel Saget/AFP via Getty Images; pp6-7 Wikipedia Commons; pp8-9 Jeff Pachoud/AFP via Getty Images; pp10-11 Michael Steele/Getty Images; p12 Chris Graythen/Getty Images; p14 Michael Steele/Getty Images; p15 Stephen Platt/Getty Images; p16 Bryn Lennon/Getty Images; p17 Jeff Pachoud/AFP via Getty Images; pp18-19 (main image) Michael Steele/Getty Images; p19 (inset) Bryn Lennon/Getty Images; p20 (top) Alex Broadway/Getty Images; p20 (bottom) Chris Graythen/Getty Images; p21 Bettman/Getty Images; p23 Stockphoto-graf/Alamy Stock Photo; pp24-25 Tim de Waele/Getty Images; pp26-27 Luc Claessen/Stringer via Getty Images; p28 (inset) Wikipedia Commons; pp28-29 Dario Belingheri/Getty Images; pp30-31 Alex Broadway/Getty Images; pp32-33 Thomas Samson/Getty Images; pp34-35 Tim de Waele via Getty Images; pp36-37 (main image) David Ramos; p37 (inset) Wikipedia Commons; p39 Chris Auld/Future Publishing via Getty Images; pp40-41 (main image) Tim de Waele/Getty Images; p40 (inset) Wikipedia Commons; p43 Chris Auld/Future Publishing via Getty Images; pp44-45 (main image) Dario Belingheri/Getty Images; p45 (inset) Justin Snetterfield/Getty Images; p47 Bryn Lennon/Getty Images; pp48-49 (main image) Chris Graythen/Getty Images; p49 (inset) Marco Bertorello/Pool/AFP via Getty Images; p51 Bas Czerwinski/Getty Images; pp52-53 (main image) Marco Bertorello/AFP via Getty Images; p52 (inset) Luc Claessen/Getty Images; p55 Yong Teck Lim/Getty Images; pp56-57 (main image) Emil Helms/Ritzau Scanpix/AFP via Getty Images; p57 (inset) Michael Steele/Getty Images; pp58-59 Alex Broadway/Getty Images; pp60 (inset) Bernard Papon/Pool/Getty Images; pp60-61 Tim de Waele/Getty Images; pp62-63 Jean Catuffe/Getty Images; p65 Stephane Mahe/Pool/AFP via Getty Images; p67 Tim de Waele/Getty Images; p69 Tim de Waele/Getty Images; p70 Reuters/Alamy Stock Photo; p71 Reuters/Alamy Stock Photo; p73 Manuel Blondeau/Corbis via Getty Images; p74 (inset) Tim de Waele/Getty Images; p75 Szymon Gruchalski/Getty Images; p76-77 Dario Belingheri/Getty Images; p79 Chris Graythen/Getty Images; p81 Marco Bertorello via Getty Images; p81 Dario Belingheri/Stringer via Getty Images; p83 Jorge Luis Alvarez Pupo/Getty Images; p85 Stuart Franklin/Getty Images; pp86-87 Thomas Samson/AFP; p89 Lionel Bonaventure/AFP via Getty Images; p90 Lionel Bonaventure/AFP via Getty Images; p93 Tim de Waele/Corbis via Getty Images; p95 Tim de Waele/Corbis via Getty Images; p97 Action Plus Sports Images/Alamy Stock Photo; p99 Randolph Images/Alamy Stock Photo; pp100-01 Jens Otte/Alamy Stock Photo; p103 Marco Bertorello/AFP via Getty Images; p105 Wikipedia Commons; p107 Lars Ronbog/Frontzone Sport via Getty Images; p109 Belga News Agency/Alamy Stock Photo; p111 Philippe Lopez/AFP via Getty Images; p113 Reuters/Alamy Stock Photo; p115 Luc Claessen/Getty Images; p117 Roger Viollet via Getty Images; pp118-19 Wikipedia Commons; pp120-21 (main image) Wikipedia Commons; p120 (inset) AFP via Getty Images; p121 (inset) Wikipedia Commons; pp122-23 (main image) AFP/Getty Images; p123 (inset) Roger Viollet via Getty Images; p125 (top) Gilbert Lundt; Jean-Yves Ruszniewski/TempSport/Corbis/VCG; p125 (bottom) AFP via Getty Images; p127 (top) Gilbert Lundt/Jean-Yves Ruszniewski/TempSport/Corbis/VCG; p127 (inset) Reuters/Alamy Stock Photo; p128 Franck Seguin/Corbis/VCG via Getty Images; p129 Pascal Rondeau/Allsport; p130 Wikipedia Commons; p131 Joel Saget/Getty Images; pp132-33 (main image) Tim de Waele/Corbis via Getty Images; p133 (inset) Bryn Lennon/Getty Images; pp134-35 Jesse Wild/Procycling magazine via Getty Images; pp136-37 Thomas Samson/Getty Images.

Every effort has been made to acknowledge correctly and contact the source and/or copyright holder of each picture and Sona Books apologises for any unintentional errors or omissions, which will be corrected in future editions of the book.